PLANNING YOUR CAREER

Written by two college placement officers who have helped find positions
for thousands of graduates, this practical book offers you concrete
assistance in selecting your career goal, finding the right job, and
achieving career success. Specific, proven suggestions tell you how
to organize your job campaign, locate potential employers, make the
most of company training programs, develop professional stature.

PLANNING YOUR CAREER

ROBERT CALVERT, JR.
Manager, Student and Alumni Placement Center
University of California, Berkeley

JOHN E. STEELE
Commerce Placement Director
College of Commerce and Administration
The Ohio State University

McGRAW-HILL BOOK COMPANY, INC.
New York   San Francisco   Toronto   London

This book is set in Century Schoolbook, a typeface that belongs to the Century family of types. Century Roman, the original face, was cut in 1895 by Linn Boyd Benton in collaboration with Theodore Low DeVinne. Century Schoolbook was designed for maximum legibility in schoolbook printing.

The chapter titles and exhibits are in News Gothic.

90MUMU7987

To all college graduates who seek
success in their careers and to their
college placement officers

PREFACE

This book is designed for the college student or graduate, to help him launch his career and progress in his chosen field. It is intended as a career planning guide to which our colleagues in the college placement field may refer their students. While the book is directed to the college student or graduate, the principles outlined apply to employment seeking also at the professional level.

Graduation from college does not ensure success in a career. Too many graduates of all ages are not using their talents or their investment in a college education effectively. The job dissatisfaction, reduced income, and general frustration of these graduates reflect the penalty for their failure in career planning.

Although much has been published on occupations, job seeking, and careers, this is the first book written especially for the college graduate by two college placement officers. The experience of thousands of students and alumni, employers, faculty members, and placement officers is brought together in this volume. The result is a systematic presentation of principles important in the three key phases of career planning. Part I, "Selecting Your Goal," details the process of self-inventory and the procedure for equating assets and interests with career alternatives. Part II, "Organizing Your Job Campaign," presents a four-step formula for the successful job campaign, which is essential in launching a career. Part III, "Evaluating Your Progress," discusses problem stages in career development, with particular emphasis on periods crucial to success, and develops techniques for measuring career progress.

Despite the many sources of assistance available to him, the college graduate must personally assume the major responsibility for his progress in career selection. At the same time he should benefit from the experience of those who preceded him. Learning everything from personal experience is costly in time. As Henry Ford said, "The school of experience is the best school, but by the time you graduate you may be too old." We have tested the action steps presented in this book during the past fifteen years, and are convinced that the reader who follows the approach outlined will materially improve his chance for success.

The economic aspects of a college education should not be overemphasized. Vocational training is not the primary objective of colleges and universities. Their function is to prepare young men and women for continuing intellectual growth, for responsible leadership in society, and for living within themselves with a sense of dignity and personal satisfaction. These broad objectives are realized, however, only when graduates are economically and personally satisfied with their work.

We appreciate the encouragement of our many colleagues in the college placement and personnel recruitment field who cooperated in the preparation of this book. Special thanks should go to Joan Fiss Bishop, Director of Placement, Wellesley College; Eugene W. Dils, Director, University Placement Service, University of Oregon; B. Keith Duffin, Director of Placement, Brigham Young University; Frank S. Endicott, Director of Placement, Northwestern University; Robert F. Herrick, Executive Director, College Placement Council; and J. Douglas Snider, Director of the Bureau of Personnel Relations and Placement, Indiana University. Valuable assistance was also provided by Samuel M. Beach, Beach and Hunt; John H. Handy, Handy Associates; Thomas W. Page, Institute of Government and Public Affairs, University of Illinois; Donald Robbins, Twelfth Civil Service Regional Office; Sam N. Wolk, U.S. Civil Service Commission; and others who are cited in the text. Expert help in typing and preparing the manuscript was provided by Mrs. Glynda Eaton, Mrs. Janet Moore, Mrs. Janet James, and Mrs. Grace Lee.

Finally, our deepest appreciation goes to our wives and children who have put up with "the book" during many winter evenings and summer vacation days.

ROBERT CALVERT, JR.
Berkeley, California

JOHN E. STEELE
Columbus, Ohio

CONTENTS

99600

PART ONE: SELECTING YOUR GOAL

CHAPTER 1

CAPITALIZE ON YOUR COLLEGE TRAINING

A century ago fewer than 2 out of every 10,000 Americans held a college degree. College and university graduates usually entered law, medicine, or the ministry. Today 44 out of every 10,000 Americans hold a college degree—a figure double that of twenty years ago. The great increase in the number of academic degrees awarded in recent years is evident from Exhibit 1.

Graduates enter over a thousand occupations. A college degree opens the door to many careers. However, it no longer guarantees success. It does guarantee opportunity. Opportunities today are greater. So is the competition. The importance of selecting the correct career path is greater than ever.

College training contributes to your development in ways which cannot, and should not, be measured in dollars and cents. But on a financial basis alone, your education may be one of the soundest investments you could make. Statistics indicate that as a college graduate you may earn from $300,000 to $700,000 during your career, as against $200,000, the probable lifetime earnings of a person without college training. Quite a few who read this book may become millionaires, at least in terms of lifetime earnings. Statistics support the value of education at every level (Exhibit 2).

Clearly, although a college education has no cash surrender value, it is the best insurance policy you could own. It is an

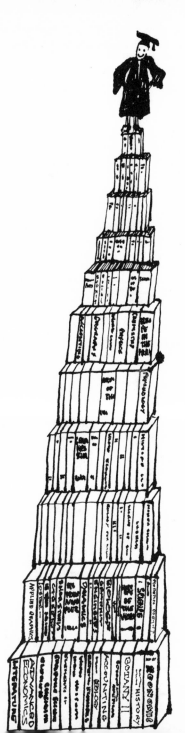

investment which you will utilize each year after graduation. But it is a sizable investment. Consider what you are spending: four years of your life, to begin with; the $12,000 you might have earned during four years; an amount totaling perhaps $7,520 for tuition, books, room, board, and travel. College endowment funds or state appropriations contribute $4,000 more to finance your college training. This brings the total to $23,520—the cost of a house, all the automobiles in a typical dealer's showroom, or a small fleet of pleasure boats.

The cost of training for your job may include in addition an amount readily and willingly invested by an employer. Recruiting, selecting, and training a single college graduate may cost an employer from $3,000 to $20,000.

IMPORTANCE OF COLLEGE TRAINING

Your education is important to our economy. In an age of growing specialization, the employer depends upon college graduates to keep his organization healthy. He needs the new products developed by college-trained researchers, the increased productivity stemming from talented market research and skilled salesmanship.

Your education is also important socially. Cities and towns depend upon college graduates for leadership. Successful school boards, United Fund campaigns, PTAs, scouting organizations, social welfare agencies, and political organizations usually have college graduates as their nuclei. Most colleges and universities were originally chartered to improve the geographical areas where they are located by training men and women to make significant economic, cultural, social, and civic contributions. That purpose has not changed.

Through your college training, you have grown in two important ways.

Academically, through classroom lectures and discussions, laboratory assignments, term papers, and independent research, you have acquired the knowledge and skills you will use for the rest of your life not only to earn a living, but also to

Exhibit 1 ACTUAL AND ESTIMATED NUMBER OF DEGREES AWARDED DECENNIALLY, 1869-70 TO 1969-70

ACADEMIC YEAR	BACHELOR'S	MASTER'S	DOCTOR'S	ALL DEGREES
1869-70	9,371	—	1	9,372
1879-80	12,896	879	54	13,829
1889-90	15,539	1,015	149	16,703
1899-1900	27,410	1,583	382	29,375
1909-10	37,199	2,113	443	39,755
1919-20	48,622	4,279	615	53,516
1929-30	112,484	14,969	2,299	129,752
1939-40	186,500	20,731	3,290	216,521
1949-50	432,058	58,183	6,633	496,874
1959-60	401,000	75,700	9,700	486,400
1969-70	709,000	138,900	18,100	866,000

Source: Louis H. Conger, Jr., and Marie G. Fullam, "Prediction of Earned Degrees to 1969-70," U.S. Office of Education Publication, September, 1959.

learn how to live. You have acquired a general and professional fund of knowledge. You have learned logical approaches to the situations and problems of life.

Personally, through such nonclassroom extracurricular activities as professional societies, sorority, fraternity, or dormitory activities, departmental clubs, publications, and athletics, you have acquired social intelligence and the ability to get along with others and to adjust to many different types of people. As a student, you have learned how to chair meetings, plan political campaigns, monthly programs, and bulletins; you have learned how to get work done through committees, and how to persuade others to follow your ideas. All these skills are important for personal happiness and essential to vocational success.

College training, however, must be properly harnessed to be of value. A college degree does not of itself provide the necessary vocational direction. College graduates frequently flounder, changing jobs and direction, with consequent personal and financial dislocation. As the opportunities increase, so do the chances of making a wrong choice. The wider the choice of jobs, the more important career planning becomes.

Career planning means far more than job hunting. It does not mean looking haphazardly or taking the path of least resistance and settling for the job most easily located. The National Cash Register Company has published a booklet on salesmanship entitled "Your 100,000 Hours." This number of hours is a rough estimate of the amount of time that you will spend working—a strong suggestion that you plan in advance for such a large segment of your life.

Career planning is similar to the designing required to build a house. If you were thinking of building, you would first discuss your ideas with family, friends, or builders, and then reduce your thoughts to writing. The blueprint for your proposed dwelling would minimize the possibility of error and simplify making changes as the construction progressed. The blueprint for your house would be your long-range plan. The solving of problems that arise during the building, in conversations with the architect or contractor, would constitute your short-range

Exhibit 2 LIFETIME EARNINGS IN RELATION TO EDUCATION

One to three years of elementary school	1.00
Eight years of school	1.40
One to three years of high school	1.63
Four years of high school	1.98
One to three years of college	2.43
Four years of college	3.33

Base: One to three years of elementary school = 1.00.

Source: Herman P. Miller, "Annual and Lifetime Income in Relation to Education," American Economic Review, December, 1960, p. 981.

plans. The two together would increase the likelihood that the final product would meet your expectations.

The concept of manpower planning at long-range is increasingly important to employers too. After World War II, many firms were shocked at their lack of potential executives. The cessation of hiring during the depression of the 1930s and the manpower shortage of the war years had made impossible the development of understudies for key executives. Many organizations were in fact forced to sell out or combine with others because they lacked the skilled top management needed to continue alone.

The pressure for additional management personnel has forced organizations to take and maintain a more complete inventory of their available manpower, develop superprograms for producing better executives in less time, and observe more closely the performance of embryo executives. Before World War II, most employers used a short-term "job approach" to obtain executives. An applicant was hired for a job and either worked his way up or didn't. In this way the less able people eventually were left behind. The survival-of-the-fittest method produced some executives in thirty years. Today employers cannot wait so long. They too have to plan, look ahead, and develop their potential.

Experience with many college graduates indicates that a twenty-year career plan for the beginner is the most intelligent approach. Twenty years from now, you will have arrived at the peak of your career. After that, what happens to you professionally will be conditioned by those first twenty years.

The beginner faces a multitude of paths and possibilities. If it were possible for you to go up in a helicopter and take aerial photographs of your possible career paths and their destinations, you could quickly find your goal and select the best route toward it. This is not possible. Guidance helps; faculty, parents, placement counselors, employers, and others will offer counsel. But the final responsibility for a decision is yours.

THREEFOLD APPROACH TO SOUND CAREER DEVELOPMENT

Experience with thousands of college graduates indicates that career planning should cover three important phases: selecting a vocational goal, organizing a job campaign, and evaluating your career as you progress.

1 Selecting your goal You must know what you are and what you have to offer before you can begin to think about where you are going. An inventory of your qualifications and interests will suggest the most logical fields for you, with your particular combination of talents and interests. Once you know the fields for which you are best suited, you can begin to decide which types of employment best meet your abilities and needs.

2 Organizing your job campaign It takes technique and skill to find a suitable position, and you will need to use both for this purpose over and over again. At a twenty-fifth reunion, Harvard graduates discovered that "less than 5% of us who took jobs on leaving college have stuck to them to the present."* The average 1936 Yale graduate held 3.12 positions during the first fifteen years after his graduation.†

The following four-step formula for a job campaign has been successfully used by many college graduates:

Step 1: Assemble your tools. Developing effective job-hunting tools is preliminary to your campaign. What should you

---

* John R. Tunis, *Was College Worthwhile?* Harcourt Brace and Company, Inc., New York, 1936, p. 17.

† John Hersey, "Yale '36—Look at Them Now," *Harper's Magazine*, September, 1952, p. 24. Taken from *History of the Class of 1936, Yale College: Fifteen-year Record.*

include in your resume?* Should you develop a portfolio? How can you tailor your letters of application to meet employers' needs?

Step 2: Locate potential employers. Careful research is needed to find the employers most likely to satisfy your present and future needs. This means careful study of many organizations before you begin to make contacts. Then, what references should you use? How can your college placement office help you? What are the roles of private employment agencies and executive-search firms?

Step 3: Contact prospective employers. The correct approach requires finesse, not merely enthusiasm and good intentions. When should the letter of application, the resume, or a telephone request be used to obtain an interview appointment? How should you apply for civil service positions? What does the employer look for in the interview? How should you prepare for it? Intelligent interviewing with the right employers is the climax of your job campaign.

Step 4: Follow up employment prospects. How do you follow up the interview without becoming a nuisance? How important is a visit to the employer's place of business and how do you make the best use of it? How can you handle several job offers simultaneously? What yardstick should you use to decide which to accept?

3 Evaluating your progress This phase of career planning comes after you have accepted the right job. Good per-

* The word "resume" is taken from the French *"résumé"* and is pronounced *rez'zu may'.*

Exhibit 3 KEY PERIODS IN CAREER DEVELOPMENT

Adapting to the training period
Achieving "professional" status
Preparing for the crucial thirties

sonal analysis, sound career selection, and a systematic and successful job campaign have served to launch your career. Talking with alumni—both successes and failures—has focused attention on the following key periods in career development (Exhibit 3).

First, of course, is the *training period.* What goals should you set for yourself in this period? How can you supplement the formal training program? A good start in your career is just as important as a good start in a college course.

Early achievement of full *professional status* or recognition of your competence and proficiency will accelerate your career. How do you develop yourself for future promotions? What is the role of further training in this phase? How do you evaluate your own progress?

During the period of the *crucial thirties,* how do you develop a professional or management point of view? When should you change positions and/or employers? Are your career goals accurate?

The acid test will come twenty years after graduation, when you can look back on your career and decide whether you have had one year's experience twenty times, or whether your twenty years' experience represents progress and success.

CHAPTER 2

WHAT CAN YOU OFFER EMPLOYERS?

"The happiest and most successful person," according to Mark Twain, "works all year long at what he would otherwise choose to do on his summer vacation." If you enjoy your job, your chances for success are excellent. And you will enjoy your work if it makes full use of your interests and aptitudes.

First, of course, you must inventory these interests and aptitudes. Every graduate can profit from Socrates's advice: "Know thyself." Kenneth Norton, placement director for the College of Arts and Sciences at The Ohio State University, makes this comment: "The trouble with most college graduates is that they do not know the answers to three basic questions: (1) What do I want to do? (2) What can I do? (3) What is there to be done?"

PERSONAL INVENTORY

Just as a salesman must know thoroughly the product or service he is going to sell, so you must know your product—yourself. Begin by detailing your qualifications and interests (Exhibit 4). Include both your own evaluation and the comments of others. Don't expect to complete your inventory in a half hour or in a single sitting. Think about it over a period of time.

Begin by listing your education, starting with the most recent and working back. Include the name of each college and its location, type of degree, major subjects and scholastic rank, and date of graduation.

Take your list back through high school. Then analyze. Which were your best subjects? Did they fall into groups, such as scientific subjects as opposed to language skills? Did your scholastic achievement in favorite subjects match your interest?

Next, review your work experience—full-time, part-time, summer, and volunteer. List each position, including your duties. Then consider what you learned from your jobs. Can you name specific skills or capacities gained through the experience? What about your performance? Did you handle some duties more efficiently—and with more pleasure—than others? Did you display initiative? Which duties did you dread, and do you know

why? Where do you feel that you fell down? Experienced candidates have a head start, especially if they can assess their accomplishments objectively. Men with military service should note their branch of service, rank, dates, and key assignments. Analyze your tour of duty to determine what was learned or done that might be of value to prospective employers.

Interests and hobbies tell a great deal about you. List them all, including activities for which you have not yet had sufficient time. Group similar things together to see what they indicate about your direction and viewpoint. Do they show that you prefer to work with your hands, with numbers, or with people? Are you happier with

Exhibit 4   CHECK LIST FOR A SELF-INVENTORY

EDUCATION
  Schools attended
  Best subjects
  Most interesting areas of study
  Academic achievement, both general and specific

EXPERIENCE
  Number and types of jobs held
  Skills and capacities acquired
  Record of performance
  Areas of interest
  Areas of efficiency

INTERESTS AND HOBBIES
  Your choices of recreation
  Extracurricular achievements—publications, research,
    awards, offices

APTITUDES
  Verbal
  Numerical and scientific
  Problem-solving ability
  Executive and organizational

LIMITATIONS
  Military service obligations
  Physical health

ideas or with things? Do you prefer work with detail, or would you rather plan a project and let someone else complete it? What are your hobbies, and what is your recreation? List your choices of entertainment, which you make absolutely freely, and you will begin to get the picture of yourself as others see you. Include any other items which might be of special interest to an employer or which are important to you. Perhaps you have written for publication, completed some significant research, received an honor or award, or developed unusual competence in a particular area.

One young woman who lacked a vocational goal turned to her placement director for assistance. Her director learned that she had not only visited forty-seven states but had spent enough time in each to know something about its attractions, products, history and traditions. For a twenty-one-year-old, she was a veritable travel encyclopedia! Her placement director helped her plan a job campaign which resulted in a position with a travel agency. Years later, she still considers her job more recreation than work.

Aptitudes should be a determining factor in career selection, for they suggest the areas where you may hope to achieve real mastery. Consider your ability to express yourself in both writing and speech, your numerical and scientific skills, your problem-solving ability, your organizational and supervisory skills, your ability to work under pressure. Take notes on how you think you stand in these areas and capacities; then add the opinions of others.

Leadership aptitude and capacity is important to employers. Do you have the ability to make decisions, teach and train others, plan things so that they are accomplished before deadlines, work well under pressure, assume responsibility and delegate some of it to others, and, most important, motivate others to want to work for and with you?

Examine your extracurricular activities.

Were you elected to responsible positions in student organizations? Were you a key worker or a popular leader? Did you prefer to lead—or to follow someone else's direction? Employers are most impressed with the ability to get results through others. They ask what you have learned from your student organizational and leadership experiences, what initiative, resourcefulness, and forcefulness you displayed, what your group accomplished during your tenure, and your standing with the group at the conclusion of your term of office. Note the specific evidences of your leadership, and be sure to include the results.

Sometimes there are clear-cut limitations and obligations that must be faced. The most obvious is the military service requirement for men. Prospective employers want to know a man's military status. Some organizations will make career offers despite impending service, but placement officers know that graduates are more employable if they are able to work at least six months before entering service.

Physical health may affect career plans. Be honest in your self-appraisal, for frankness now will help to prevent misplacement. Match your physical capacities with job requirements. Different jobs and different organizations make different demands. For instance, one girl rated herself as being in excellent physical condition, yet she left a position in a leading department store because she could not take the walking and standing. Had she analyzed herself more carefully, or had she tried retailing on a summer or internship basis, she would have recognized the problem and gone into another field.

PROFESSIONAL ASSISTANCE

Supplement your own thinking with outside help when you reach the point of diminishing returns in your self-analysis. Most large institutions have a separate counseling and testing service where trained psychologists and counselors can review your inventory, suggest additions and revisions, and outline the basic fields which would best utilize your combination of interests. As Professor Hoppock of New York University states, "One of the counselor's responsibilities is to help the student to discover both his assets and his liabilities, to accept those which cannot be changed, and to make wholesale emotional, educational, and vocational adjustment to them."* Such centers usually serve students free of charge and may also assist alumni and the general public on a fee basis.

In smaller colleges, counseling and testing are frequently combined with the placement program. If your school has neither a placement bureau nor a counseling center, ask the dean or chairman of the psychology department for other sources of assistance.

You may find the assistance you require from a public vocational counseling center. The names of reputable vocational counseling agencies may be obtained from your psychology department or placement office. Be sure to request the names of agencies especially interested in vocational guidance counseling. Another useful source is the *Directory of Vocational Counseling Services*, published by the American Personnel and Guidance Association, 1605 New Hampshire Avenue, N.W., Washington 9. Individual copies sell for $1.50.

Don't overlook the assistance you may receive from faculty members. Every student should develop close contact with one or two professors, counselors, or deans during his college career. This is as important on a campus of 500 as on one with 20,000 students.

Your faculty adviser may help you to formulate your career plans. Having observed your participation in practical or group situations, he may have a particu-

larly helpful picture of your assets and interests. He may also be able to provide helpful information on employment opportunities in his field.

Later, when you actually apply for a position, you will probably want to use faculty members as references. Permission should always be requested before listing anyone as a reference, but a single request should cover the use of a name in an entire job campaign. Many graduates err in assuming that faculty contacts will remain useful automatically throughout their careers. Nothing could be further from the truth. For best results you may wish to "jog the memory" of a reference by giving him a short written summary of your background and achievements.

There has been increasing use of psychological tests in vocational selection in the past two generations. These tests may verify your own analysis or reveal additional information about yourself. An estimated 20 million Americans take 60 million tests each year. You can't purchase these tests in a store; they are sold only to professionally trained counselors. Furthermore, to be of real value, test results should be interpreted by trained psychologists.

Most vocational counseling is based upon a battery of tests selected to provide multidimensional information. Test batteries are developed to answer specific problems faced by the candidate. Tests are chosen from five major types: intelligence, achievement, aptitude, interest, and personality. Intelligence tests measure an individual's capacity for mastering problems; they are often referred to as IQ tests. Achievement tests measure the extent of an individual's knowledge or skill in a particular subject. Aptitude tests measure a candidate's ability to acquire new information and skills, as well as his speed in so doing. Interest tests reveal a pattern of likes and dislikes. Personality tests indicate a candidate's emotional stability and personal adjustment. (Exhibit 5.)

* Robert Hoppock, *Occupational Information,* McGraw-Hill Book Company, Inc., New York, 1957, p. 284.

Any or all such tests may be helpful to a career candidate in finding direction. But they are not infallible. As Greenleaf says, "there is no test or battery of tests that will reveal the one occupation you are best fitted for. In choosing a career you will find no magic formula or test to help you. Batteries of psychological tests may prove helpful as indicators of aptitudes and abilities in certain broad fields of work—as, for example, professional, clerical, or skilled fields."*

* Walter James Greenleaf, *Occupations and Careers,* McGraw-Hill Book Company, Inc., New York, 1955, p. 86.

Exhibit 5 TESTS USED IN VOCATIONAL COUNSELING

TYPE OF TEST	MEASURES	EXAMPLES
1. Intelligence	Capacity for mastering problems (generally referred to as IQ or intelligence quotient)	Wonderlic Personnel Test Otis Self-administering Tests of Mental Ability Wechsler-Bellevue Scales of Mental Ability
2. Achievement	Extent of knowledge or skill in a particular subject	Iowa Placement Examinations Typing or shorthand examinations College midterm or final examinations
3. Aptitude	Facility and speed with which new information or skills may be learned	Army General Classification Test Purdue Pegboard Minnesota Clerical Test
4. Interest	Pattern of likes and dislikes in various activities	Kuder Preference Record Strong Vocational Interest Blank
5. Personality	Emotional stability and personal adjustment	Bernreuter Personality Inventory Minnesota Multiphasic Personality Inventory Thurstone Temperament Schedule

Do not be disappointed if you fail to make high scores in all the tests. The important thing for career planning is the profile—your pattern of scores. This is what will help you to decide where to turn.

DETERMINING YOUR ASSETS

Having analyzed yourself, pro and con, you know your liabilities and assets. Before you apply for a job, you must begin to think of your liabilities as assets. Consider such common weaknesses as "inexperienced," "too young," or "a follower, not a leader." Look at them from a positive standpoint. Present lack of experience might be thought of as flexibility. The inexperienced person can absorb an employer's procedures without having to unlearn past experiences or habits.

Employers may consider you too young for their work. You may be able to demonstrate by your past accomplishments, your ambition, your willingness to learn, and your record of hard work that you are not too young.

Are "followers" doomed by the current emphasis on developing future leaders? The answer should be an emphatic "No," as the ability to follow intelligently and resourcefully is an asset which should be of interest to most employers. Even at the top of the organizational pyramid, some following is necessary. A disgruntled college graduate called on an old family friend who happened to be president of one of the country's largest railroads. The graduate complained, "I never had a chance to lead or operate independently in any of my jobs. How do I get to your level where I may freely use my leadership skill?"

The railroad president retorted, "The higher you go, the more following you do and the more people are watching to make sure that you are following. I have to follow most of the recommendations of my operating supervisors and staff consultants, and I am constantly aware that my actions may be reviewed and criticized by my board of directors, our stockholders, or the general public."

Graduates may face the problem of low scholastic records. They are in good company. Thomas Edison, Louis Pasteur, Charles Darwin, Leo Tolstoy, Honoré de Balzac, Walter Scott, and Winston Churchill—all had indifferent scholastic records. Nevertheless, most employers favor candidates who rank high in their graduating class, and usually a good academic record correlates with later financial success, despite the occasional shining exceptions that prove the rule. One study divided graduates into four categories and computed the income for each group. They ranked from high to low income as follows: the "Greasy Grinds," the "Big Men on Campus," the "All-round Students," and "Those Who Just Sat There."*

If your grades are poor, don't search for excuses. Rather, examine your qualifications for some qualities which make grades less important.

A young man found that his scholastic record would be a handicap in starting his career in advertising. He had obtained B's in only three college courses—English Composition, Principles of Advertising, and Advertising Copywriting. He had rated A for "Advertising man" and a B for "Author-journalist" on the Strong Vocational Interest Blank. He decided that his best approach would be to demonstrate his ability to express himself through his application letter. His interest scores were incorporated into his letter as evidence that he had obtained outside confirmation of his skills.

A girl had to work her way through college, and her scholastic record showed the result. But her career inventory stressed practical experience in retailing, her chosen field, stated why she found this industry

* Ernest Havermann and Patricia West, *They Went to College,* Harcourt Brace and Company, New York, 1951, p. 164.

challenging, and emphasized the steady upward curve of her sales results.

Married students with families can usually balance work experience or family responsibilities against their low academic record. Some vividly present the ingenious methods they developed to squeeze into twenty-four hours sufficient time for classes, studying, work, rest, baby-sitting, and occasional social activities. Such a description of budgeting time shows prospective employers a great deal about a student's maturity, flexibility, sense of responsibility, and initiative.

Most applicants have many good qualities. The problem is recognizing which of these qualities are of interest to prospective employers.

CHAPTER 3

WHAT IS YOUR VOCATIONAL OBJECTIVE?

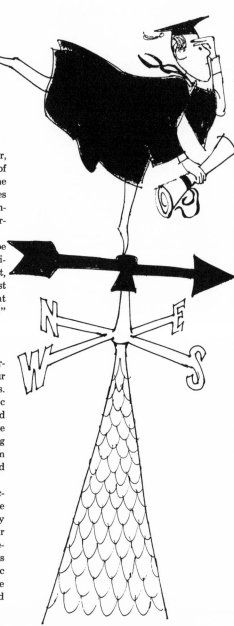

When it came time to select a career, young Benjamin Franklin took a series of walks with his father. On these walks he was able to observe at first hand all types of work available in the eighteenth century. His choice was simple, as few alternatives existed.

Career selection in the 1960s must be made from more than 30,000 kinds of positions. No wonder selection is difficult. Yet, as Thomas Carlyle stated, "It is the first of all problems for a man to find out what kind of work he is to do in this universe."

IMPORTANCE OF AN OBJECTIVE

The occupation you choose will determine the kind of life you will lead, your mode of living, and your circle of friends. Only a few generations ago, basic economic needs—the need for food, shelter, and clothing—were pressing. Today, we have added to the basic requirement of making a living demands such as satisfaction from a sense of service, professional status, and specific geographical preferences.

Whenever possible, occupational objectives should be determined during college years. Students planning professional study must select their objective early in their college careers so as to take academic prerequisites. For those who do not have plans for postgraduate study, the academic choice is much more difficult. Some of the larger universities offer over two hundred majors. A general vocational objective helps to narrow or focus the choice.

Many students elect liberal arts majors. This background is good preparation for hundreds of careers, provided that the liberal arts student develops both an academic major and a vocational goal. The major may be English, history, or political science; the vocational goal may be retailing, personnel, or teaching. The important thing is that liberal arts students develop a goal. The major, in itself, is not enough.

Many liberal arts students complicate their planning by searching exclusively for career fields suggested by their college major. Few liberal arts graduates with only the bachelor's degree will be able to work in the specific area covered by their major. One study revealed that only 1 per cent of all English majors and 6 per cent of all social science majors were employed after graduation in fields directly related to their majors. Liberal arts graduates, regardless of major field, are able to work successfully in many occupations.

The problem is not to find a job, but to find the occupational field which will best utilize your training, talents, and interests.

HOW TO STUDY OCCUPATIONS

A self-inventory (see Chapter 2) should provide a general idea of the kinds of things you can do and like to do. A similar analysis of various occupations will help you to find out what there is to be done.

Occupational brochures and monographs are available in career guidance libraries and placement offices. They provide specific and helpful information, but their life expectancy is not more than five years. From current publications, you can conduct your own survey.

The National Vocational Guidance Association recommends that occupational descriptions contain the definition, history, and current trends of the occupation, as well as its importance to society and other fields. Regularity of employment, number of people involved, and their location should be clear. Distinctive aspects of a vocation such as the age, sex, special skills, training, education, and experience of its members are also important. Lines of promotion, opportunity for advancement, and earnings and benefits should also be covered. (Exhibit 6.)

Occupational Literature by Gertrude Forrester, published by The H. W. Wilson Company, lists occupational pamphlets and where they may be obtained. Several pamphlet series are also available. The Careers Research Monographs, published by the Institute for Research, 537 South Dearborn Street, Chicago 5, covers over 224 occupational fields. The New York Life Insurance Company's series of pamphlets may also be helpful. These are distributed through the Career Information Service, Box 51, Madison Square Station, New York 10. In addition, Mademoiselle Magazine has published numerous articles on careers for women. Reprints may be obtained through the Alumnae Advisory Center, Inc., 541 Madison Avenue, New York 26.

Most libraries and placement offices have career books available. One of the most helpful may be *The Twenty-minute Lifetime: A Guide to Career Planning,* written by Gavin A. Pitt and published by Prentice-Hall, Inc. It provides pertinent information about careers in many fields. Another good source is *Career Planning* by Leonard J. Smith, published by Harper & Brothers. Much of the data is alphabetized by field of interest for easy reference.

Several excellent books are specifically slanted to the college woman and designed to present the growing number of career possibilities open to her. An especially authoritative report is *The College Girl Looks Ahead* by Marguerite Wykoff Zapoleon and published by Harper & Brothers.

Federal agencies have compiled occupational material; a complete list of publications may be obtained from the U.S. Government Printing Office. Individual bulletins may be ordered at a nominal charge, either from the individual agency or from the U.S. Government Printing Office, Washington 25. The *Occupational Outlook Handbook*, published by the U.S. Bureau of Labor Statistics, summarizes employment opportunities in a number of fields. Copies are available in placement offices, counseling centers, and libraries.

In addition, you may take advantage of the personal knowledge of faculty members and their contacts in their field. You may also learn much by talking with people employed in the fields you are considering.

Professional and trade associations often have written material concerning occupational possibilities. (See Chapter 7 for lists of other helpful source material.)

Personal experience, your own first-hand knowledge of a field and your reaction to it, resulting from a field trip arranged for a class or by a student organization, is probably the best introduction. Such visits provide an opportunity to observe and to meet managers who can answer questions. (For example, one large can manufacturer invites prospective employees to spend an eight-hour day in one of his plants before

Exhibit 6 COVERAGE RECOMMENDED BY THE NATIONAL VOCATIONAL GUIDANCE ASSOCIATION FOR OCCUPATIONAL SURVEYS

1. History of the occupation
2. Importance of the occupation and its relation to society
3. Duties: Definition of the occupation; nature of the work
4. Number of workers engaged in the occupation: number, distribution, trends
5. Qualifications: Age, sex, special qualifications or skills, scores on tests for employment, legislation affecting the occupation
6. Preparation: General education, special training, experience
7. Methods of entering
8. Time required to attain skill
9. Advancement: Lines of promotion, opportunity for advancement
10. Related occupations
11. Earnings: Beginning wage range; wage range of largest number of workers; maximum, median and average salary; annual versus life earnings; regulations; benefits, other rewards
12. Conditions of work: Hours, regularity of employment, health and accident hazards
13. Organizations: Employees, employers
14. Typical places of employment
15. Advantages and disadvantages not otherwise enumerated
16. Supplementary information: Suggested reading, trade and professional journals, visual aids, other sources, list of associations, firms, or individuals who may provide further information

Exhibit 7   CAREER PLANNING DURING COLLEGE

Freshman year: Preselection of occupation.

Sophomore year: Year of decision. Check validity of choice.

Sophomore year vacation: Tryout work in field of choice.

Junior year: Stick with choice, if valid. If not, change, but apply rigid test.

Junior year vacation: Tryout work in field of choice.

Senior year: Year of proof and action. Make definite contact with occupation and prepare to enter it.

Graduate school: Only when necessary for professional or special training.

they act on an offer. A few who cannot tolerate the noise withdraw their applications, and both candidates and employer are spared a problem.)

During college you may have the opportunity to hold short-term jobs, thus increasing your personal knowledge and experience and bringing your long-term plans into focus. One of the best outlines for utilizing personal experience is presented in *Blueprint Your Career.**

During the freshman year, you should make a preliminary vocational selection. The sophomore year might be called the year of decision, when you check the validity of your choice by tryout work in the field. If the choice is valid, stick with it. If not, think through a change during your junior year. During vacation, you may continue with advanced experience or try another field. The senior year is the time for action, when a student may begin to make a final decision, definite contacts, and specific career preparations. Graduate school should be considered when necessary for specific professional goals, but not without well-formulated plans. (Exhibit 7.)

In your preliminary planning, consider some problems which have proved stumbling blocks for many.

* Robert F. Moore, *Blueprint Your Career,* The Stackpole Company, Harrisburg, Pa., 1949, p. 21.

Is money a major objective? Some graduates err by overemphasizing the financial aspects of career planning. A study of approximately 3,300 alumni from seven different schools and colleges of The Ohio State University showed that graduates who placed income as their primary objective actually earned less than those who emphasized other criteria. Some, on the other hand, ignore money, assuming that even the most modest position provides a high standard of living, after the fashion of Hollywood movies.

Does the job offer challenge? William James said that "life is only meaningful when it is lived in response to a great challenge." This need not necessarily mean discovering new medicines, leading expeditions up the Amazon, or building skyscrapers. But it does mean that if a job is to be satisfying, it must seem worthwhile to you and utilize your abilities.

Have you checked future prospects? Career planning should include economic futures. Automatic data processing machines, for example, are making many jobs obsolete. Sixty per cent of a chemical company's present business comes from products which were not even discovered ten years ago. A classic story is that of the sales manager speaking to the board of directors of a manufacturing company. Looking at the downward sales curve, the

99600

sales manager said, "I can't understand it—our firm makes the finest buggy whips in the world."

Ideally, career planners should search for growth fields as an investor does. Consider, for example, our current trends, with electronics a major growth industry. In 1870, it was the railroad industry; in 1890, steel manufacturing. But by 1920, it was automobiles, and in the last decade we have moved into the electronic age. Your personal success will vary with, and in the direction of, your chosen field. (Exhibit 8.)

Are you aiming for the right level? Our greatest satisfactions come from doing a job well. Most of us know when our work is poor, average, or outstanding. For maximum personal happiness, select an occupation in which you will be one of the best in your field. You will be happier, and more effective as an outstanding teacher than as a poor school principal, a good medical technician rather than a mediocre doctor, or a fine salesman instead of a frustrated sales manager. This doesn't mean stamping out your ambition, but it does mean realistically assessing demands of various positions.

Reality must not be limited to your own self-assessment. You must appraise opportunities realistically too. A counselor spent weeks helping a senior select his vocational goal. Early one morning the student walked into the counseling office. He had made his decision. He had picked his career on the basis of a newspaper story describing the working-capital shortage which affects small contractors. This senior planned to purchase bulldozers, mobile cranes, dump trucks, and similar heavy equipment and rent them out on a daily basis to contractors. His proposal looked good on paper. The only catch was that he didn't have the $1 million working capital necessary to enter this business on a profitable scale. Unrealistic planning is as bad as no planning at all.

Reality also says—and sometimes harshly—that women should plan too.

Young women face unpredictable futures, according to Joan Fiss Bishop, director of placement at Wellesley College. A woman's career may become the pivot for her life, combined with marriage and family, or given up either temporarily or permanently. Reilly also points out that many women never do marry, that husbands are not always able to be the breadwinners, and that a vocational interest may be helpful, if not essential, in the years after a family is grown.* Greenleaf points up the importance of a working woman's financial contribution to the education of children and to the standard of living of the entire family.‡ In addition, young women today *want* to work—to earn, to contribute, to attain professional status and satisfaction. Increasingly, regardless of time out for home responsibilities, women need career planning.

Are you patient? Long-range goals are rarely achieved immediately. They may have to give way temporarily to intermediate steps, interim positions. The potential tax expert may first have to gain experience as an auditor, cost accountant, financial analyst, property accountant, or budget analyst. The feature writer may begin his

* William J. Reilly, *Life Planning for College Students,* Harper & Brothers, New York, 1954, pp. 65-66.
‡ Walter James Greenleaf, *Occupations and Careers,* McGraw-Hill Book Company, Inc., New York, 1955, p. 86.

Exhibit 8 MAJOR GROWTH FIELDS

1870	Railroad industry
1890	Steel manufacturing
1910	Banking and finance
1920	Automobile industry
1930	Labor relations, recreation
1940	Toll-road planning, plastics
1950	Electronics

career as a reporter or copywriter. Similarly, sales experience provides a helpful background for market research.

An interim position may help those who are still uncertain to learn more about their vocational skills or provide helpful contacts with potential employers. Typical interim jobs are assistant to the manager of a chamber of commerce, promotional staff member of a trade association, or assistant college placement officer.

Sometimes beginners underestimate the importance of their job and their own achievement. They might take encouragement from a vocational counselor who said, "Every vocation is big if you do it better than it ever was done before; dignify your vocation by excellent performance."

CHAPTER 4

WHICH EMPLOYERS FIT YOUR PROGRAM?

The final step in defining your vocational goal is to analyze employers in general, by industry or service, size, geographical locations, and other major features. Later you will want to search out organizations with suitable specific openings.

GENERAL TYPES OF EMPLOYERS

There are thousands of different types of employers. Your approach will be easier if you group them by general categories. The *Standard Industrial Classification Manual,* published by the U.S. Bureau of the Budget, lists the ten major types of employers in the United States:

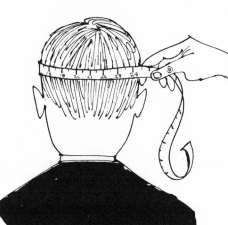

1. Agriculture, forestry, and fishing
2. Mining and extractive
3. Contract construction
4. Manufacturing
5. Transportation, communications, and public utilities
6. Wholesale and retail trade
7. Finance, insurance, and real estate
8. Service industries
9. Government
10. Establishments not elsewhere classified

Each major type may be broken down, as in the following analysis.

The agriculture, forestry, and fishing classification includes farming, nurseries, hunting and trapping, horticultural services, timber tracts, fishing and fishery services.

The mining and extractive group includes mining metals, coal, crude petroleum, and natural gas, and quarrying of stone, sand, gravel, clay, gypsum, ceramic, and refractory minerals.

Construction covers building, repairing, and improving of private and commercial structures, highways and streets, and waterworks.

Manufacturing is an extremely diversified classification, with twenty-one major divisions and employers, ranging in size from the gigantic petroleum refining and chemical industries down to the one-plant, small-staff operation of a printer or toy manufacturer. These employers are engaged in such industries as foods, textiles and apparel, lumber, wood, paper products, and the production of machinery ranging from huge metal presses down to minute optical instruments.

Transportation, communications, and public utilities are usually placed in one category. Transportation includes — for both freight and passengers — railroads, ships, trucks, buses, airplanes and underground pipe lines. Communications includes telephone, telegraph, radio, and television. The public utilities group contains employers engaged in electric and gas operations, water supply, sanitary services, steam companies and systems, and irrigation systems.

Wholesale and retail trade includes distributors for industrial and consumer products—building materials, general merchandise, food, automobiles, apparel, furniture—whose outlets range from gigantic chains to small specialty shops.

The finance, insurance, and real estate classification includes banks, personal and business credit institutions, investment houses, insurance companies and salesmen, and real estate brokers.

Major service areas are recreation, from bowling alleys to theater; health, from hospitals to medical laboratories and organizations; education, including museums, schools, libraries, nonprofit organizations

of civic, social, and other groups. This classification also includes personal services such as photography, hairdressing, and repairs of all types and business services such as professional accounting, employment and advertising agencies, and news syndicates.

The government group includes agencies of Federal, state, municipal, and international governments. All positions compensated from public funds fall within this classification. These include civil service workers, policemen, firemen, elective or appointive political officials, and teachers and administrative personnel in the public school systems from elementary schools through state universities.

STUDY OF SPECIFIC EMPLOYERS

The first step in narrowing the field is to select the most logical general group. A readily available source of assistance, with information more specific than that given in occupational brochures, is the literature that employers prepare for college graduates. Such material, which describes the employer's business, his job opportunities, and employment advantages, is available in most college placement offices. While each presentation depicts one organization only—and usually in a favorable light— it does provide a general idea of career opportunities in the employer's field. Excerpts from several employer publications seeking to attract talent are given in Exhibit 9.

LARGE VERSUS SMALL EMPLOYER

Every placement officer repeatedly hears applicants say, "I don't want to work for a large organization," or "I wouldn't be happy teaching in a small school." Fortunately, there is room for both preferences. Each has advantages and disadvantages which should be evaluated.

For example, while large employers often offer more promotional opportunities

Exhibit 9 EXCERPTS FROM TYPICAL EMPLOYER DESCRIPTIONS

LEVER BROTHERS COMPANY

"Lever Brothers Company is engaged in a highly competitive industry in which its leadership depends upon the ability to develop, produce, advertise, and sell huge volumes of its well-known products. These tasks are carried out by a streamlined corporate organization built around three marketing divisions: Lever, Pepsodent, and Foods. Each of these divisions consists basically of two operations: product advertising and merchandising and a field sales organization.

"The Company has a standing policy of personnel promotion from within this marketing framework.

"Because of the close relationship in all phases of Lever's marketing operations, field sales training is essential as a prerequisite for all marketing management; and managerial experience is begun as early as possible.

"Long-range career progress within the marketing area is based on continuing evaluation of each man's abilities, interests, and job performance at each stage of development."

INTERNATIONAL BUSINESS MACHINES CORPORATION

"IBM is a leader in the exciting and growing field of electronics, computation and automation. . . . We intend to maintain leadership in data processing systems, for civilian and military use, and in business machines of all types. . . . You may find that you have abilities and talents, as yet untapped, which will change your course. This is possible within IBM because our personnel policy is based on a respect for and consideration of the individual. We encourage progressive planning, technical ingenuity, and creative thinking."

UNION STARCH AND REFINING COMPANY, INC.

"The company is looking for men who will not be content with the old way of doing things but will constantly seek improved or new methods; individuals who believe their security lies in their own value to an organization and their ability to make themselves an asset to the company. . . . I believe I can safely say that you will work harder with this company than you would with many others. . . . Union Starch and Refining Company is large enough to have a complex, varied and diversified business but small enough and flexible enough that the newly hired individual can get a comprehensive picture of corporate operations in a relatively short period of time."

25

SEARS, ROEBUCK & COMPANY

"Sixty-five percent of this country's total expenditures is spent on consumer goods and services. Obviously, those businesses engaged in the distribution of consumer goods are going to continue expanding at a tremendous rate. . . . Sears is the *sixth largest corporation* in the United States, the *world's largest general merchandiser,* doing over $4 billion worth of business a year, employing more than 200,000 people. . . . Sears is looking for college men of executive caliber:

"men who are eager to accept responsibility

"men who can deal with people

"men who can make intelligent decisions."

BOARD OF EDUCATION, POMONA, CALIFORNIA

"Five citizens comprise the Board of Education for the Pomona Unified School District. It is the announced policy of this board to 'maintain for the children of Pomona a better-than-average school system with respect to scope, quality, school plant and equipment, and personnel.' To implement this policy, the district seeks well-trained, qualified teachers.

"The administration believes that the most effective professional services can be rendered by teachers in a democratic organization. It is the intent, therefore, to institute democratic procedures in all approaches to the solution of our educational problems."

BURDETT OXYGEN COMPANY

"The Company was formed in 1923, beginning its existence as an organization with six employees and one small oxygen producing plant. Today Burdett ranks among the top seven in the country as a producer of gases for industrial use. Future prospects for Burdett products appear unlimited as new uses arise each year in countless fields. With this situation, the only future for Burdett is one of forward growth and progress. But growth requires a team, and Burdett needs able, aggressive salesmen to contact a vast field of prospective buyers."

NATIONAL AERONAUTICS AND SPACE ADMINISTRATION

"The National Aeronautics and Space Administration is an independent civilian Government agency established October 1, 1958.

"Broadly, NASA's mission includes all matters pertaining to the civilian space and aeronautical research activities of the Nation. Included are not only research but also the development, construction, testing, and operation for research purposes of aeronautical and space vehicles, manned and unmanned, together with related equipment, devices and components.

"NASA's work includes basic and applied research for the expansion of human knowledge of phenomena in the atmosphere and space; the improvement of the usefulness, performance, speed, safety, and efficiency of aeronautical and space vehicles; the development and operation of vehicles capable of carrying instruments, equipment, supplies, and living organisms through space; and the preservation of the role of the United States as a leader in aeronautical and space activities."

AMERICAN HOSPITAL SUPPLY CORPORATION

"Few industries offer such an assured growth prospect, coupled with relative immunity from general economic recessions, as the medical and health field.

"America's hospitals currently spend $8.3 billion a year for goods and services—$2.7 billion for non-payroll items. In spite of phenomenal growth of hospitals since World War II, twice again as many hospital beds as there now are will be needed by 1975!

"The recognized leader in supplying this field with everything from beds to bandages is American Hospital Supply Corporation, with a 30,000-item product line (ever-growing through research). Founded in 1922, the Company has tripled in size during the last 10 years alone and annually sells more than $145 million in hospital and laboratory equipment and supplies."

SHELL OIL COMPANY

"Thousands of men and women graduating from college have resolved the question of finding the right position with the right employer by joining Shell.

"Shell is part of the oil and chemical industries which employ directly more than a million persons and indirectly support many millions more. The oil and chemical industries are essential to our national security, to industry and commerce and to the community at large. Petroleum and gas, for example, provide approximately 75 per cent of our nation's energy.

"The size and diversity of the Shell Companies afford a chance to learn and grow. They offer a great variety of activities and unusual opportunities for the new employee as he gains experience and demonstrates his individual worth. Key positions are held by employees who have come up through the organization, a result of Shell's policy of 'Promotion from Within.' "

and greater security and fringe benefits, small employers may offer greater prominence for an outstanding person, more opportunity to benefit from the growth of the organization, and the possibility of eventual ownership. A large company may require transfers and relocations, while a small company will not. A large organization will probably provide more extensive and more scientific training, but a small employer may offer responsibility more quickly. Some of the advantages of working for a large and for a small employer are listed in Exhibit 10.

THE ROLE OF COMPROMISE

College graduates often look in vain for the "perfect job." Actually, it doesn't exist. Compromise is inevitable. Similarly, high school seniors selecting a college usually compromise their criteria on size, location, and cost.

Location often forces a compromise. Most beginning jobs in geology, for example, start in field locations, regardless of the applicant's preference. By contrast, the graduate entering on an advertising career usually works in a large metropolitan area. One young graduate who wanted very much to enter the field of personnel accepted a position in a small mining town, even though both he and his wife preferred urban life.

Health often affects or dictates geographical location. You may need a certain climate, have reasons for living near your family, or have other personal requirements. One graduating senior came into the college placement office excited about an "ideal" job offer. During a discussion of the position, the placement director asked the student whether he had considered personal items such as religious opportunities, as the young man took his church affiliation very seriously. In seeking an answer to this question, the senior learned that his nearest church would be 65 miles distant. He decided he was not interested in settling so far away from his church.

Often graduates must compromise on the type of position they accept in order to enter the field of their choice. In the advertising field, many college-trained persons begin in the mail room. Prospective college teachers may start at the high school or junior high school level. Industrial relations majors heading toward labor negotiation may start their career as economic statisticians.

Most graduates prefer positions which permit the maximum evening time for family life. Unfortunately, in many positions evenings are not free. Much of the work of the life insurance salesman is done in the evening, for example. Retailing usually involves evening and Saturday work, especially just before Christmas.

OPPORTUNITIES FOR OVERSEAS POSITIONS

College graduates have many mistaken notions about employment opportunities in other countries. Some graduates have heard that high salaries are paid for overseas work and seek it to make a fortune. Other graduates assume most positions are in glamorous foreign capitals. Consider seriously the following features of overseas employment.

Many foreign countries have passed laws restricting the numbers of Americans permitted to work in their country. This legislation often limits the number of Americans to a small percentage of the total employees in an organization. In other cases, the only Americans admitted are those with skills not possessed by nationals of the country. This often limits employment of Americans to persons having experience in a specialty, such as geological exploration or sanitary engineering.

If you go abroad for your career, you should think in terms of twenty to thirty years, not two or three. You are going for your vocation—not to enjoy a vacation.

Exhibit 10 ADVANTAGES OF LARGE AND OF SMALL EMPLOYERS

LARGE EMPLOYER	SMALL EMPLOYER
More job levels, therefore greater promotional opportunities.	Person of ability may stand out sooner and more prominently.
Greater potential earnings.	May offer eventual ownership possibilities.
Starting salary often higher.	Advancement often faster; competition may be less.
More extensive training programs.	Quicker assumption of responsibility and more immediate assignment to a specific job.
Greater security and fringe benefits.	More opportunity to benefit from growth of the organization.
Greater financial strength to weather depressions and technological changes.	Individual may be able to give more direction to work of organization and more readily see results of his own efforts.
Promotion from within policies enable graduate to make career with one employer on a lifetime basis.	More willing to hire older, experienced graduates.
More staff resources available to help solve problems as they arise.	Often greater opportunity for the independent person who works best alone.
Greater expenditures on research to ensure progress.	Work is often more varied and not as routine.
Diverse operations permit functional and geographic transfers.	Little need for geographical relocation, upsetting family life and friendships.
Often more scientific approach to management.	Policies and procedures more flexible; individual initiative may be more encouraged.
Less danger of being merged with large employer because of financial difficulties, competition of new products, or uneconomical size.	Often get better experience if you are interested in going into business for yourself.
More scientific promotion policies; little danger of relatives being favored as in a family-owned business.	Easier identification with goals of employer; more apt to be known by top management.

Your value to your employer will increase with your knowledge of the people, language, customs, and thinking of the country or area in which you work. It is uneconomical for employers to train you for an overseas assignment if you plan to return to the United States in a short time.

The glamour and novelty of strange lands may wear off, and an overseas position may become like any other job, only far away from home. Don't count on an overseas assignment to an enticing foreign capital. You may dream of spending warm April evenings at a sidewalk café along the rue de la Paix. If you accept an overseas position, you may find yourself spending those evenings in a desert oasis, second class.

Men with families should pay particular attention to overseas problems that may be faced by their wives and children. In some countries social contacts with other people may be limited. Health conditions, educational opportunities, and even potential danger to women and children should be examined.

The income received from overseas positions may not be as attractive as it appears. If salaries are higher than in this country, living costs may be even higher relatively. Americans are expected to maintain a certain standard of living overseas which may be higher than their level in this country.

In many countries, Americans become members of a minority group—a role which may be strange and unique to the average United States citizen. Foreign nationals do not always think favorably of Americans, and may indeed be hostile. This places a particular burden of adjustment on Americans in these countries.

Unless you have language aptitude and are flexible enough to adjust to other cultures, a career in a foreign country may not be desirable for you. Two semesters of a foreign language is hardly sufficient preparation for a career in a given country.

There is tremendous competition for positions abroad. Both Federal government and private business organizations are swamped with applications for positions abroad. Applicants need both language competence and technical qualifications to merit serious consideration.*

You have analyzed yourself, done preliminary review of the variety of occupations, and planned a general goal. Now you can become specific and begin to plan a job campaign. As you make contact with employers and consider individual jobs, your long-range plans should fall into clearer focus. In planning, emphasize where you are going, not where you are at the moment. As Charles Kettering said, "My interest is in the future, because I'm going to spend the rest of my life there."

* One of the best discussions on overseas employment appears in "Pros and Cons of a Foreign Career" in *Foreign Operations*, published by Foreign Operations, Inc., New Haven, Conn., 1958. A copy may be available in your placement office.

PART TWO:
ORGANIZING
YOUR JOB CAMPAIGN

Step 1 ASSEMBLE YOUR TOOLS

CHAPTER 5

SUMMARIZING YOUR QUALIFICATIONS

Following the selection of a vocational target, the next phase of sound career development is planning a successful job campaign. You must first prepare the tools you will need. Begin by considering the resume, the portfolio, and the employer application blank.

THE RESUME

A resume is an individually designed written summary of personal, educational, and experience qualifications intended to demonstrate fitness for a particular position or positions. More briefly, a resume is a digest of your qualifications for a job. The resume is often referred to as a personal data sheet, a personal profile, a statement of qualifications, or an experience record. It often serves as the keynote of the job campaign.

Once a rarity in job campaigns, the resume has become a tool used routinely by skilled job seekers. Fifteen years ago, the applicant who sent a resume with his letter of application received compliments on his unique informational enclosure. Today, wide use of the resume means that only an effective one will be helpful.

The resume *differs in principle* from the standard application blank used by employers. A resume focuses attention on your strongest qualifications and develops them in light of the peculiar demands of the position for which you are applying. By contrast, an application blank usually

covers, without any special emphasis, all aspects of a candidate's background.

For example, a resume might include academic average for a prospective teacher, whereas a candidate for a recreation position might omit any reference to his scholastic record. Candidates often include their grade point average when it is high, but omit it if their record is poor. Application blanks usually request scholastic information from all candidates.

Resumes are developed individually and no two are exactly alike. However, most include (1) identification of the candidate, (2) summary of qualifications or goals, (3) personal data, (4) educational history, (5) employment record, (6) military service (if pertinent), and (7) references.

The resume should start by *identifying the writer*. It is best to repeat, even though they appear on the accompanying letter, your address and phone number. Your name should appear at the top of the page or in another prominent place. Identifying information may be given as follows:

Ralph W. Browning
109 Concord Street
Manchester, New Hampshire

Home phone: 724-4313
Office phone: 724-2300, ext. 629

A photograph helps to personalize your resume and makes it easier for the employer to remember you after the interview. Usually, this is a head shot. Application-size photographs may be purchased from specialized firms for 5 cents each in orders of twenty-five or more. Copies are made from originals. Some firms are Klick Photos, Union City, Indiana; Portrait Copy Company, Sunny Slope Station, Kansas City, Kansas; and the Minneapolis Photo Company, Box 1158, Berkley, Michigan. In some cities and states, Fair Employment Practices laws prohibit employers from requesting photographs. In other areas, candidates may not voluntarily sub- mit an application photograph. You should check local laws with your college placement officer.

Increasingly, resumes begin with a short *summary of career objectives* and qualifications, which furnishes an immediate impression of the candidate. Such a statement frequently summarizes both the short and long-range goals of the candidate.

"Young woman with professional training and a genuine interest in teaching seeks first-grade position in a Central Illinois public school."

"Trained industrial engineer interested in a position utilizing both management and technical skills."

"Liberal arts graduate with production experience desires appropriate position with a manufacturing company."

"Advertising executive with ten years of diversified and successful account experience seeks position with large organization offering ownership possibilities."

"Sales manager or assistant sales manager position sought by young college graduate with successful public relations and sales training experience."

Most resumes include such *personal data* as date of birth (not age, as this changes), height, weight, health or physical limitations (if any), marital status, and dependents.

A number of other items could be used in the personal section, depending on the position sought. For example, an overseas birthplace might be helpful to an applicant for an overseas position. Citizenship is important to organizations doing defense work, as they must limit employment on classified projects to United States citizens. Father's occupation is appropriate if you wish to demonstrate a family tradition in a profession. Special skills, such as languages, hobbies, travel, and machine skills, may present important side qualifications for a position. Community activities may demonstrate civic responsibility or leadership skills. In some instances a wife's special education or work experience may be of interest.

Educational history is usually summarized. Start with the highest degree received and work back to the name and location of your high school. Elementary school need not be listed. Colleges and universities attended should be included along with their location (if it is not obvious), dates of attendance, degrees awarded, and major courses of study. Students often include their grade-point average or class rank, if known. Alumni who have been out of school five or more years omit this information, as their work performance provides a more appropriate indication of ability.

Many graduates dwell excessively on the fact of college training. This they share with millions of others; special qualifications need emphasis. These may include campus honors and activities which demonstrate professional interests, leadership, participation, and accomplishment. It is preferable to list and describe significant contributions to three organizations rather than to cite ten groups in which you merely held membership.

The summary of *employment* becomes an increasingly important part of the resume as your career develops. If you use the chronological approach, the record should include employer's name and address, type of business or industry, length of employment, title of position and nature of duties, with particular emphasis on assignments pertinent to your current interest, and reason for leaving.

Men and women who have earned a significant part of their college expenses should note this on their resume. Summer work may be summed up by a phrase such as "During the last two high school and the first two college summers I worked in canneries, summer camps, and on a construction job." However, summer work pertinent to career goals should be described in more detail.

Military service may be summarized in the same way as employment and should include your branch, dates of active duty, rate or rank, duties or assignments, and your current selective service or reserve status. Military experience need not be described unless it is pertinent to your job interests, such as Navy electronics experience for electrical engineering or an Army finance background for accounting. Leadership responsibilities in the services should also be mentioned.

More and more resumes omit a list of *references,* simply stating, "References will be furnished on request." However, many authorities still recommend using them. If references are included, they should be varied. Ideally, people whose names are used should be at the same professional level as the potential employer, but you must of course pick people who are familiar with your capabilities.

Employers feel that three types of responsible community leaders usually make poor references. Clergymen often concentrate on ethical or moral standing rather than on employment assets and liabilities. Physicians and dentists are acquainted with your physical health, but not your vocational potential. Politicians know many people, but few of them well enough to give a specific reference; also, politicians avoid negative remarks.

References should be listed completely, and a consistent style should be used. The proper form includes name, title, organization, and address:

> Mr. Albert G. Brown
> District Sales Manager
> Allegheny Water Company
> 525 North Scranton Street
> Allentown, Pennsylvania

You may wish to separate your references to indicate how each knows you. An experienced salesman listed his references under the following headings:

I worked for these people.
I sold to these people.
These people have known me for more than ten years.

IMPROVING YOUR RESUME

One of the ways in which almost any resume may be improved is by *slanting it to the employer's need*. This requires an appreciation of his point of view. What type of person does he favor? What specific skills and experience does he need? If you can answer these questions, you will be able to select and slant the appropriate material from your background.

Slanting also involves interpretation. You may suggest to the employer what your background means to him. A sales candidate with experience as a restaurant counterman during college would probably not mention his knowledge of sandwiches and sundaes. Rather, he would stress the various types of people he met. If he were applying for a position as an accountant, he might emphasize what he learned about the financial problems of small businesses.

You should be sensitive to the tone of resumes in your occupation. Engineers or scientists often list their professional interests and backgrounds in a detailed and straightforward fashion. Public school administrators frequently include their philosophy of education. Men seeking advertising positions often make their resumes a demonstration of their creativity.

Avoid unnecessary data. Care must be taken to eliminate data not of interest to the employer, such as color of eyes, name of elementary school, or father's birthplace.

If salary information is included, some employers may assume you are too high priced for them or that you are not "heavy enough" for a key position. The best procedure usually is to talk to the employer and let him judge your worth to him.

A good resume is brief and concise. One page should be sufficient for new graduates. Sentences should be short and to the point. Your language, grammar, and spelling will be on display. Don't confuse the reader by excessive use of abbreviations. It is much more comfortable to read "University of Minnesota" than to be faced with "Univ. of Minn." "Cambridge, Ohio," is much more accurate than "Cambridge, O.," as O. might be misinterpreted to mean Oregon or Oklahoma.

John Hardwick's first resume (Exhibit 11) is filled with unimportant data, poorly slanted, too spread out, and unnecessarily outlined. It forces the reader to decide what he wants to do.

In the revised resume (Exhibit 12), John Hardwick (1) emphasizes vocational objective; (2) omits or reduces data which fail to support his objective, such as the names of his elementary and high schools and extracurricular activities; (3) builds up pertinent academic study and helpful work and military experience to support his vocational objective; (4) avoids over-labeling or excessive outlining, which serves no useful function and detracts from more important material; (5) provides home address and phone number; (6) presents more helpful references and indicates their positions; and (7) places the resume on a single page with a more artistic layout.

Consider a *functional approach*. Most resumes summarize employment and educational history in chronological fashion. This clarifies the date of each experience.

A functional approach emphasizes vocational skills or specialized knowledge rather than the details of a number of positions. It may even omit the names of employers and the dates of employment. The functional resume may be developed by an applicant who wishes to spotlight his skills rather than his frequent job changes. It is particularly helpful in a field in which job

Exhibit 11   JOHN HARDWICK'S FIRST RESUME

John C. Hardwick
Southwestern University
Tulsa, Oklahoma

I. PERSONAL DATA

    a. Age—25
    b. Height—6 feet, 1 inch
    c. Weight—175 pounds
    d. Health—excellent
    e. Birthplace—Osgood, Oklahoma
    f. Marital status—married, no children
    g. Church affiliation—Presbyterian

II. EDUCATIONAL BACKGROUND

    a. Osgood Elementary School, Osgood, Oklahoma, 1945-1949
    b. Osgood High School, Osgood, Oklahoma, 1949-1953
    c. Electrician's School, U.S. Navy, 16 months, 1954-1955
    d. Southwestern University, Tulsa, Oklahoma, 1957-1961
        B.S. in Electrical Engineering, June, 1961
        College average, 2.4 (A = 4; B = 3; C = 2)

III. WORK EXPERIENCE

    A. Part-time Work
      1. Office boy, Johnson Realty Co., Osgood, Oklahoma—two summers, 1952, 1953
      2. Soda clerk, Osgood Drug Store, Osgood, Oklahoma—two summers, 1956, 1957
      3. Assembly line worker, Del Ray Electrical Company, Tulsa, Oklahoma—three summers, 1958, 1959, and 1960
    B. Full-time Work
      Electrician's Mate, Third class, U.S. Navy, 1953-1957

IV. ACTIVITIES

    a. High School
        Dramatics Club
        Boy Scouts
        Science Club
        Varsity football and basketball
        Lettermen's club

b. College
   Public Affairs Forum
   Intramural Sports
   Phi Alpha Chi Fraternity, Assistant Pledge Trainer during Junior Year
   Y.M.C.A.
c. Extra-school
   Masonic Lodge
   Reading
   Sports

V. REFERENCES

a. Harlan Van Anderstine, Minister, Osgood, Oklahoma
b. Captain J. R. Waters, U.S.S. Midway, c/o F.P.O., San Francisco, Calif.
c. Mr. Ora M. Humble, Burning Prairie, Oklahoma

Exhibit 12 JOHN HARDWICK'S REVISED RESUME

John C. Hardwick
2814 East Eleventh Street
Tulsa, Oklahoma
(243-5698)

PHOTO

VOCATIONAL OBJECTIVE   Engineering position utilizing interest and training in the electrical power industry

PERSONAL

Birth date: September 6, 1935   6' 1"; 175 pounds
Married; no children   Health: excellent

EDUCATION

Southwestern University, Tulsa, Oklahoma, B.S., June, 1961
    Majored in electrical engineering, including courses in special problems of
    public utilities, electrical circuitry, commercial transformers, industrial
    switches, public utility management, and consumer economics.
U.S. Navy Electrician's School, 16 months (1954-1955)
    Specialized in electrical circuits, transformers, and switches.
Osgood High School, Osgood, Oklahoma—diploma, 1953
    Majored in college preparatory course.

WORK EXPERIENCE

Assembly line worker, Del Ray Electrical Company, Tulsa, Oklahoma, summers of
    1958, 1959, and 1960—Learned construction details of the T-3, T-4, and
    T-5 commercial transformers used by 85 per cent of all public utility plants
    in Oklahoma and Texas.
U.S. Navy, 1953-1957—Primary duty assignment was 28 months spent as an
    Electrician's Mate on the U.S.S. Midway. Directly responsible for maintenance
    and immediate repairs on ship's lighting system.
Held a variety of summer and part-time jobs in high school and college.
Was 100 per cent self-supporting during college.

REFERENCES

Mr. George L. Jones   Professor L. R. Bordan, Chairman
Chief Engineer   Electrical Engineering Department
Del Ray Electrical Company   Southwestern University
1734 South Sheridan   Tulsa, Oklahoma
Tulsa, Oklahoma

            Professor Ira J. Brown
            Electrical Engineering Department
            Southwestern University
            Tulsa, Oklahoma

Exhibit 13 WILLIAM STEUBEN'S RESUME

William S. Steuben
1843 Los Altos Drive
Los Angeles 24, California
(911-8429)

PHOTO

VOCATIONAL OBJECTIVE   Personnel Director, preferably in a heavy manufacturing company

PERSONAL BACKGROUND

Born: April 26, 1920
Married, three children
Health: excellent

Whittier College, BA (Economics), 1941
UCLA, MBA (Personnel), 1948
Veteran, no reserve status

EXPERIENCE (some of it concurrent)

Recruiting: experienced in employment interviewing (4 years) and supervision of hiring section (1 year).

Job Analysis: Developed and utilized job descriptions in employment hiring (2 years).

Employee Counseling: Counseled in military induction and separation centers (4 years) and have had heavy employee counseling responsibility throughout career.

Training: Completed the 18-month training program for a major manufacturing corporation before entering military service. Later helped develop two employee training programs and assisted with the curricula of others.

Safety: Served as assistant plant safety engineer (6 months).

Wage and Salary Administration: Conducted comparative salary surveys among heavy manufacturing companies (2 years) and developed and initiated formal salary review procedures.

Labor Relations: Assisted in gathering and preparing data for contract negotiations and participated in labor-management conferences (3 years). Served as employer representative on grievance committee (1 year).

CURRENT SALARY $12,000 plus bonus

References and other information will be supplied upon request.

changes are frequent, such as high school teaching. William Steuben's resume (Exhibit 13) is organized functionally.

Stress *eye appeal.* Care should be taken to design a resume artistically. It should have eye appeal and appear uncluttered. Barbara A. McDonald's resume (Exhibit 14) emphasizes eye appeal and readability.

Should each resume be personally typed or may resumes be reproduced mechanically? Several years ago the answer would have definitely favored the personally typed resume. Today, however, resumes are so commonplace that employers are more concerned with content than method of reproduction. The time saved by mechanical reproduction may be spent in developing a more effective resume or in contacting additional employers. Multilith or offset printing equipment usually produces neater work than mimeograph or spirit process machines.

Resumes may be improved with *advice from employment experts* (personnel men, placement officers, or professional acquaintances). Most people are pleased to give advice, which Mark Twain described as "the world's easiest gift." If possible, seek more than one outside opinion, but exercise judgment in deciding which advice to accept.

Some organizations specialize in professional resume construction. However, if you study resume design and seek outside advice, you can usually design just as effective a resume on your own. Furthermore, if you develop your own resume, it will certainly have a personal style.

If you are planning an extensive mail campaign, conduct a "trial run" by sending out a few resumes for employer reaction. Few personnel officers will comment directly. However, you may sense whether their response was favorable; if it was not, your shortcomings may be indicated.

A more detailed presentation of the resume may be obtained from the book *Job Strategy* by Allan Rood, published by the McGraw-Hill Book Company, Inc., New York, 1961.

THE PORTFOLIO

The portfolio is a more extensive description and presentation of your qualifications than the resume. It may be used during the interview or mailed with a covering letter which highlights points of interest. Young college graduates in advertising, commercial art, industrial design, journalism, or architecture find the portfolio especially useful, since it may include samples of their work. It is individually prepared and used for final rather than initial or screening interviews, except when the employer and the applicant are at some distance from each other. The portfolio may be left with the employer, but should be picked up in a few days. Setting a deadline for its return may ensure that it will be read. If the portfolio is mailed, a letter that highlights special qualifications should accompany it.

Most portfolios have an attractive protective cover or binding with a title page listing the name of the applicant, his address, phone number, and vocational interests. In addition the portfolio should include a summary of your background.

There should also be a section that develops qualifications, presents examples of work, or lists accomplishments or other facts. For example, a journalism student might include clippings or a photostatic copy of a press association citation for his paper. A prospective teacher might include his college transcript, a list of scholastic honors, or a letter commending him for developing a strong fraternity scholarship program. A sales promotion expert might include a sales letter of which he was particularly proud and information on the sales increase which resulted. A factory manager might chart production increases on his last job, together with decreases in cost per unit and in plant accidents.

Exhibit 14 BARBARA A. McDONALD'S RESUME

Barbara A. McDonald
433 Race Street
South Hadley, Massachusetts
(693-2134)

PHOTO

VOCATIONAL OBJECTIVE   Position in business aspects of the publishing field offering opportunities for advancement

PERSONAL

Born: December 23, 1939	Weight: 115
Health: good	Single, no dependents
Height: 5' 6"	Typing speed: 60 w.p.m.

EDUCATION

Mt. Holyoke College, South Hadley, Massachusetts, A.B. degree, 1961
Major: English
Minor: Economics and Foreign Languages

Bronxville (New York) High School, graduated 1957

EXPERIENCE

Business Manager, "The Mount Holyoke News" during 1960-1961 senior year. Responsible for financial management and advertising sales and production. Directed staff of six. Qualified for this position through work during sophomore and junior years.

Office Assistant, Camp Evangeline, Naples, Maine, during summers of 1958, 1959, and 1960. Typed letters for Camp Director, some of which I was asked to compose myself. Kept financial statements and prepared bills. Prepared checks for signature. In general, served as the administrative assistant to the Director.

REFERENCES

Professor Franklin L. Allen	Professor Eleanor Byrd
(Adviser to School Paper)	(Faculty Adviser)
Department of English	Department of English
Mt. Holyoke College	Mt. Holyoke College
South Hadley, Massachusetts	South Hadley, Massachusetts

Miss Alice M. Overshaw
Director, Camp Evangeline
P.O. Box 19
Naples, Maine

Photostatic copies of letters of reference or commendation may be included.

Mechanically, it is helpful if the portfolio is no larger than 8½ by 11 inches, so that it will fit into a standard personnel office file. In some fields, such as commercial art, a larger size is necessary. If the portfolio is to be used extensively, individual pages should be covered with a plastic or cellophane cover to prevent smudging and create the impression that each employer is reading a summary prepared especially for him.

Once you have developed a portfolio it may serve you throughout your working career. Its contents may vary between job campaigns but your own individual style and format may help during several job searches. Alert graduates keep their portfolio in mind and save clippings, charts, and letters of commendation to use during a future job change.

One of the best descriptions of the portfolio and an excellent reference source is *Pick Your Job—and Land It* by Sidney and Mary Edlund and published by Prentice-Hall, Inc., Englewood Cliffs, New Jersey, 1954. Differences between the resume and the portfolio are outlined in Exhibit 15.

THE APPLICATION BLANK

Resumes and portfolios interest the employer in your qualifications. Before you are actually hired for a position, most employers require you to fill out a detailed application blank (Exhibit 16). This form

Exhibit 15 DIFFERENCES BETWEEN RESUME AND PORTFOLIO

RESUME	PORTFOLIO
Usually one page.	Usually several pages, in brochure or booklet form with an attractive cover or sturdy binding.
Serves as a summary (digest) of qualifications.	Presents qualifications in some detail. Frequently includes actual work samples.
Used to obtain preliminary job interviews, often mailed with application letter.	Taken to final job interviews, left with the employer for detailed study, or used in place of preliminary interview to overcome geographical barriers.
Prepared in quantity, often by use of a reproducing process.	Individually prepared.
On many campuses, required for interviews.	Seldom used for campus or screening interview.

Exhibit 16 THE APPLICATION BLANK

Qualification Record

Date __MARCH 23, 1962__

This form will usually provide all the necessary preliminary information. It may be supplemented, however, by letter or resume.

PERSONAL

PLEASE PRINT NAME

Name __JANICE__ (FIRST) __KEENE__ (MIDDLE) __DUPRE__ (LAST)

Present Address __2714 BOWIE STREET AUSTIN__ (STREET) (CITY) Zone __4__ State __TEXAS__ Phone __CA 2-4454__

Home Address __47 FEDERAL STREET EL PASO__ (STREET) (CITY) Zone __10__ State __TEXAS__ Phone __AD 4-9726__

Birth Date __DEC 23 1940__ (MO. DAY YR.) Height __5'6"__ Weight __115__ Are You a Citizen of the United States? __YES__

Single ☒ Married ☐ Remarried ☐ Separated ☐ Divorced ☐ Widow(er) ☐ No. of Dependent Children _____ Total Number of Dependents _____

MILITARY

Have you ever served in the Military Service of the United States? __NO__ Serial Number(s) __—__

Give details of service:

DATE OF INDUCTION	BRANCH	INDUCTION	RANK	DISCHARGE	TYPE OF DUTY	REASON FOR DISCHARGE	DATE OF DISCHARGE

EDUCATION

COLLEGES ATTENDED (UNDERGRAD. & GRAD.)	DATES FROM	DATES TO	DEGREE EXPECTED	DEGREE REC'D	DATE	SUBJECT OF SPECIALIZATION
UCLA	1958	1960	—	—	—	LIBERAL ARTS
UNIVERSITY OF TEXAS	1960	1962	B.A.		6/62	MATHEMATICS

UNDERGRADUATE: Attach transcript if available. Class rank (example: 10th in 100) __TOP THIRD OF CLASS (EXACT RANK UNKNOWN)__

Grade point average (Also state maximum of scale) __3.01 (4 = A)__

GRADUATE: List graduate courses by name and give grades or attach transcript:

SUBJECT OR COURSE	GRADE	SUBJECT OR COURSE	GRADE	SUBJECT OR COURSE	GRADE
—					

Foreign Languages: Speak __SPANISH__ Read __SPANISH__ Write __SPANISH__

Give titles of theses completed or in process and name of supervising professor for each

Bachelor's __PROFESSOR JOHN E. YOUNG, DEPT. of MATHEMATICS, UNIVERSITY of TEXAS__
If no thesis give name of major professor

Master's _____
If no thesis give name of major professor

Doctor's _____
Thesis subject and faculty advisor

ACTIVITIES

Campus Activities (Dramatics, Athletics, Publications) __REPORTER, DAILY BRUIN (UCLA). SECRETARY of MATHEMATICS CLUB (TEXAS)__

Honors __DEAN'S LIST (TEXAS)__

Recreations and Hobbies __READING__

% College Expenses Earned (Include Scholarships but exclude Military Service Benefits)—Undergraduate __30%__ Graduate __—__

44

EMPLOYMENT

Give past employment record as completely as possible, starting with your present or latest employer. Include summer employment. (If space insufficient list on back of this page.) For any unemployed or self-employed periods, show dates and locations.

COMPANY NAME	ADDRESS	DATE MO. YR.	RATE OF PAY	NATURE OF WORK AND NAME AND TITLE OF IMMEDIATE SUPERVISOR	REASON FOR LEAVING
1. SOUTHWEST PETROLEUM COMPANY	NO. STREET 187 FANNIN St. CITY ZONE HOUSTON 2 STATE TEXAS	FROM JUNE, 1961 TO August, 1961	$360	COMPUTER PROGRAMMING ASSISTANT MR. R. L. SCANLON DIRECTOR, COMPUTER SERVICES	RETURN TO SCHOOL
2. TEXAS WESTERN COLLEGE	NO. STREET 1000 RANDOLPH St. CITY ZONE EL PASO 8 STATE TEXAS	FROM JUNE 1960 TO August, 1960	$275	RECEPTIONIST, OFFICE of The REGISTRAR MR. E. R. FULMER ASSISTANT REGISTRAR	RETURN TO SCHOOL
3. MESA DRIVE-IN	NO. STREET 2078 N. MESA St. CITY ZONE EL PASO 9 STATE TEXAS	FROM JULY, 1959 TO SEPT., 1959	$260	COUNTER CLERK MR C. D. COATES OWNER	RETURN TO SCHOOL

RESEARCH EXPERIENCE

Describe briefly your research experience, if any.

AS A COMPUTER PROGRAMMING ASSISTANT WITH THE SOUTHWEST PETROLEUM COMPANY, I WORKED CLOSELY WITH SCIENTISTS SEEKING COMPUTER SOLUTIONS TO RESEARCH PROBLEMS.

INTERESTS

Describe briefly type of work desired. State reason for preference.

COMPUTER PROGRAMMER OR RELATED WORK. MY COLLEGE COURSES AND MY COMPUTER PROGRAMMING EXPERIENCE LAST SUMMER INDICATE INTEREST AND APTITUDE FOR THIS WORK.

REFERENCES

Give names of two persons to whom you are not related and by whom you have not been employed. These people should have known you for several years.

NAME	ADDRESS (BE SPECIFIC)	BUSINESS	YEARS KNOWN
John P. TEAR	142 TEXAS St., EL PASO, TEXAS	INSURANCE EXECUTIVE	10
William K. HENDERSON	307 MISSOURI St., EL PASO, TEXAS	SALES MANAGER	6

MEDICAL

New employees are required to pass a physical examination given by a member of the company's medical staff. Do you have any known physical impairments? __NO__ *(Examples are: loss of limb, defective sight or hearing, or ailments which you have or have had affecting the heart, lungs, muscles, or nervous or circulatory systems.) Please list.*

*Have you ever been arrested for violating any law (excluding minor traffic regulations) or been involved in a criminal offense? Yes_____ No_X_*

Have you ever been affiliated in any manner with any communist, fascist, totalitarian, or other similar organization or activity? Yes_____ No_X_ If your answer is "yes," give details on back of this page.

Will you accept employment in any part of the U. S. A.? NO *List any locations not acceptable* OUTSIDE HOUSTON AREA

State preference, if any, and reason MY FIANCE WILL BEGIN A THREE YEAR SEMINARY PROGRAM IN THE FALL. I WILL WANT TO WORK IN HOUSTON DURING THIS PERIOD

Social Security No. 172-26-027 _____ *Date available for employment* JULY 1, 1962

SIGNATURE *Janice K. Dupre*

45

consolidates in one document information of greatest interest to the particular employer.

Before you start to fill out any application blank, read the instructions. Some employers prefer to have the forms typewritten, others want the information printed, while still others desire the data in your own handwriting. Scan the entire form before you begin, because some questions may be related.

Fill out blanks carefully and completely. Many job seekers carry detailed information with them so that they will be able to list the required facts accurately and easily. If you are hired, the application blank will be placed permanently in your personnel file or may even become your master personnel record. It will be read and used many times, especially when your name comes up for promotion. Every form will include questions not pertinent to your background. It is best to respond to these with a dash, indicating that you have read the question but that it does not pertain to you. A sloppy application blank hints at careless work habits and lack of interest in the employer. The personnel director for a large missiles manufacturer recently was forced to select a few candidates for summer jobs from a large group of highly qualified engineering students. He made his initial screening on the basis of neatness and quality of handwriting on application forms.

An increasing number of application blanks have been designed by psychologists and are reviewed and evaluated by them. Typical of the items added by psychologists are questions soliciting essay responses on such topics as your attitude toward former employers, your self-concept, and your preference for various types of people. Don't attempt to outguess the psychologists; do answer questions carefully and completely. Your responses provide still another measure of your qualifications, and they help assure the prospective employer that you will fit the job's requirements.

CHAPTER 6

PRESENTING YOURSELF THROUGH THE LETTER OF APPLICATION

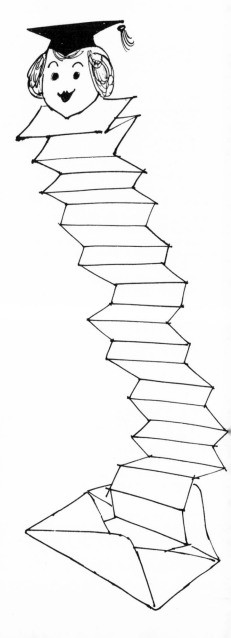

A leading automobile manufacturer requested three candidates for a personnel position. Each was asked to write a letter summing up his qualifications. The first two applicants were obviously well qualified. The third, seemingly much less qualified, was referred only because the employer had asked for three. Surprisingly, the third was the only one interviewed—and he received the job. Investigation revealed that he was chosen because of his letter. Most application letters have less dramatic results, but the importance of knowing how to apply for a position by mail cannot be overemphasized.

Your chances of landing a job solely on the basis of a letter of application are practically nil. Few employers are willing to hire a person until they have had a personal interview. The purpose of a letter of application is to introduce you to a prospective employer and to obtain an interview appointment or at least an application blank. Although the letter probably will not land a job for you, a certain impression will be created. A good letter should create the desire on the part of the reader to want to talk with you.

IMPORTANCE OF A GOOD LETTER OF APPLICATION

A well-written letter is the most efficient way to present your qualifications to a busy executive. Letters of application are read, compared, and used to screen out candidates for employment.

Personnel officers receive many letters and from more applicants than they can interview. Even the typical help-wanted ad often attracts 50 to 100 replies. To receive attention, a letter of application must be good.

A good letter of application presents your writing and organizational skills—both of which are pertinent to most positions. In addition, many candidates often find it easier to present their outstanding achievements in writing than during an oral interview.

Even if a letter does not immediately lead to an interview, it may help you. Many employers do not advertise or openly recruit, but rely on carefully screened unsolicited applications. Good letters written by likely candidates are filed for futu.e reference.

TYPES OF LETTER CAMPAIGNS

Letters may be planned for two types of mail campaigns—the "rifle" and the "shotgun" approaches.

In a "rifle" campaign, a list of employers who normally require people with your qualifications is selected, with the help of placement offices, employment agencies, faculty, and advertisements. The letters are aimed at a specific and known target.

In a "shotgun" campaign, letters are mailed to many employers in an attempt to develop or "stumble upon" openings. Names of employers for such a broad campaign may be taken from directories and trade or professional rosters.

While a "rifle" campaign is usually more efficient in time and money, a "shotgun" approach may develop more job leads. Typical was the Ph.D. candidate graduating from a western university who sought a position in a medium-sized or large university working directly for the president. Few such positions are open. Seldom are they broadcast. This candidate sent personally typed letters accompanied by a resume to 300 university presidents. From this mailing, twelve employment possibilities developed. (Note that this was only 4 per cent of the institutions contacted.) He spent several weeks visiting the prospective employers before accepting a position as assistant to the president of a Big Ten university.

CONTENTS OF THE LETTER OF APPLICATION

While all letters of application should be personalized to be effective, the best letters follow certain basic principles. Start the letter whenever possible by addressing the employment manager or department supervisor by name. Their names are usually available through placement offices, employment agencies, or directories. Or call and ask the telephone operator, but be sure to get both the name and title correctly. As a last resort, use a functional job title such as "Personnel Director" or "Sales Manager."

The *first paragraph* should attract the reader's attention, tell why the letter was written, and include formal application for the job.

Many candidates begin letters with a question.

"Does the Mid-Atlantic Publishing Company have a position for a former editor of the University of Pennsylvania student newspaper who is interested in making publishing his life's work?"

Others begin with a third-person introduction.

"Professor W. E. Holst of Willamette University suggested that I write concerning my qualifications for a position in your accounting department."

Some candidates reflect their research on the employer:

"For some time I have been studying your company, using your products and talking to your retailers. I am very much impressed with your engineering skill, sound marketing procedures, and progressive management policies."

A good introductory paragraph usually raises some questions in the mind of the reader. The *middle paragraphs* should answer them. They should indicate why you are interested in the employer and show a knowledge of his organization.

You may wish to point out how your background fits the requirements of the job. In this connection, positive statements are much more helpful than negative ones. One candidate used this statement:

"While my experience before entering the School of Business was in fields other than banking, I feel that this is no disadvantage."

This was revised to positively point out its significance to the prospective employer by saying:

"You will note that I worked six years before entering the School of Business. This experience should provide helpful background for banking, as two years were spent in factory production and four years in office management."

Three candidates presented their qualifications as follows:

"As an English major at White College, I was frequently called upon by fellow students to edit letters, posters, campaign materials, and reports. In addition, several of my compositions were printed in *With the Writers* (a monthly magazine published by the English Department) and one of my articles was accepted by a national magazine. With this training and experience on the campus, I believe I can be of assistance to your organization in your methods and procedures department, public relations department, library, or correspondence department."

"I know I can sell! Throughout my college career I have always been selling something—an idea to students in a campus organization, vacuum cleaners on a house-to-house basis, corsages for social events, and clothing in a retail store. I love the challenge of selling, the responsibility of budgeting my time, and the thrill of closing the sales order."

"I am interested in teaching in your high school because of the many favorable comments made by members of your faculty with whom I took a training institute last summer. In addition, I am personally well acquainted with your geographical area and would welcome the opportunity to live in your community."

Specific examples develop a clear and interesting picture. More effective than "I have had extensive experience in the publishing field" is "For the past twenty years I have worked for a major publishing house soliciting manuscripts, rewriting copy, and consulting on editorial policy."

If you are now employed, tell why you are seeking another position. This should be done without referring negatively to your present employer.

The letter should end with a question to prompt a response. The *final paragraph* usually requests an interview, an application form, or additional information.

If you ask for an interview appointment, it is always appropriate to suggest when, in general, you will be available for an interview. You may wish to provide your telephone number. Some candidates say that they will call the employer's secretary to schedule an interview appointment. This technique often causes friction. If an employment possibility exists, most employers will be pleased to contact you.

Many closings are improper. "Sincerely" is too informal for a business letter unless you are personally and well acquainted with the employer. "Sincerely yours," "Very truly yours," or "Yours sincerely" are preferable. Note that only the initial letter is capitalized. Do not forget to type your name. Then add your signature. Your letter is not complete without your signature.

HOW TO IMPROVE THE LETTER

Many application letters fail because of minor details. Fred Summer's letter (Exhibit 17) illustrates *correct business-letter style* and summarizes suggestions concerning content. While there are other acceptable methods, the style used here is common. The content is given as a formula deliberately, because readers tend to copy examples verbatim. By phrasing your letter in your own words, you will personalize it and get better results.

Modernists often recommend a more functional opening than the conventional "Dear Mr. McCormick."

"Good morning, Mr. McCormick!
   "May I apply for a position . . . "

"Yes, Mr. McCormick,
   "I am impressed with your company's growth . . . "

"Greetings, Mr. McCormick,
   "From Professor Bucks of the University of Vermont . . . "

These functional greetings may inject a note of freshness, but unless you know something of the personal preferences of the person to whom you are writing, a more conventional style is safer.

Trick letters fall into the same category. One letter of application was written upside down. Another had pennies pasted across the top and began "I want to be sure to get my two cents in." Still another had a burnt corner and the opening "I have a burning desire to work for your company." Such letters may bring smiles, but their value is limited to fields such as advertising, which make use of attention-getting skills.

While you may be proud of stationery imprinted with your fraternity crest or home address, a letter of application should be neatly typed on businesslike plain white bond paper. One employer measured the businesslike approach of candidates for a secretarial position by choice of stationery. First he discarded all applications written on colored paper. Next, he discarded handwritten letters. Then he culled out all letters not on plain stationery. From the remaining letters, typed on plain white paper, he made his choice. There is one error more serious than all of these—writing a letter of application on the stationery of your current employer.

A good letter is usually limited to a single page. Any additional information appears on the resume. The letter should invite reading by being easy to read; it should have generous margins, three or more paragraphs of fewer than ten lines each, and no errors, strikeovers, or messy erasures. Every letter should contain correct sentence structure and grammar.

The letter of application should be an original, not a carbon copy. One candidate sent out hundreds of mimeographed postcards in an attempt to locate a personnel job. He gave the impression of not caring enough about any particular employer to send a personal letter. Needless to say, his campaign was unsuccessful.

Planning your letter includes more than attention to correct mechanical details. Remember that you are introducing yourself.

Exhibit 17 CORRECT STYLE FOR APPLICATION LETTER AND FORMULA FOR CONTENT

Box 137
Hanover College
Hanover, Indiana
April 25, 1962

Allow two or three spaces here.

Use complete title and address.

Mr. George McCormick
Director of Personnel
American Manufacturing Company
124 South Third Street
Louisville, Kentucky

If you know the name, use it, rather than "Dear Sir."

Dear Mr. McCormick:

Opening paragraph: State why you are writing, name the position or type of work for which you are applying, and mention how you heard of the opening.

Middle paragraphs: Explain why you are interested in working for this employer and specify your reasons for desiring this type of work. If you have had experience, be sure to point out your particular achievements or other qualifications in this field or type of work.

Middle paragraphs: Refer the reader to the attached application blank or personal data sheet (which gives a summary of your qualifications), or to whatever media you are using to illustrate your training, interests, and experience.

Closing paragraph: Have an appropriate closing to pave the way for the interview by asking for an appointment, by giving your phone number, or by offering some similar suggestion to facilitate an immediate and favorable reply. Ending your letter with a question encourages a reply.

Very truly yours,

Fred A. Summers

Fred A. Summers

Always sign letters!

Top and bottom margins should be equal.

If a resume or other enclosure is used, note in letter.

Enclosure

Put yourself in the employer's position. What does he need to know?

Slanting to the employer's need is as important in the letter as in the resume. One personnel man says, "Omit everything from the letter of application which will not encourage the employer to hire you."

A good letter of application should tell what you can do for the employer. Read the letter by George Johnson (Exhibit 18). Will it arouse interest on the part of the employer? Note how little is told about the candidate's qualifications. He assumes that possession of a master's degree is sufficient qualification for a position.

By contrast, Anthony Spaulding's letter (Exhibit 19) clearly states his qualifications and develops them in terms of his field. It is basically aggressive in tone, which is intended to demonstrate enthusiasm for a sales career.

A good letter of application stresses the *interests of the reader*, not the writer. Dale Carnegie emphasized the value of thinking in terms of the person to whom you are speaking or writing. Many inexperienced letter writers suffer from a disease known as "I-itis"—excessive use of first person pronouns "I," "my," "me." I-itis reflects lack of skill in communication and detracts from the impression the applicant seeks to create with his letter.

Fortunately, I-itis can be cured by proper editing. Notice how John Young's letter (Exhibit 20) handles first person pronouns. Count them. You may be surprised to discover there are none. A letter can be written without using a single "I" or "me." However, eliminating all first person pronouns has some disadvantages. These pronouns help make a letter smoother and more natural. John Young's letter avoids "I's" but at the expense of good construction.

Professor Francis Weeks of the University of Illinois, a specialist in business correspondence, feels that the most important single aspect of a good letter of application is a *tone of modest self-confidence*. Note the letter of Theodore Page (Exhibit 21), which is an actual letter mailed to 200 employers. It violated the cardinal rule against mimeographed letters of application. Yet, thanks to its tone of modest self-confidence, it led to four job offers. Its writer is now employed on a tropical South Pacific island.

Many candidates fear duplicating resume material in the letter of application and in consequence fail to send an effective letter. *Blend the letter and the resume.* The letter must tell something about the writer and attract interest so that the resume will be read.

Review your application letter. Start by checking mechanics and style. Next, check for sales effectiveness. Review the statements which tell why you selected your field of work or feel qualified for it. Ask yourself the question: Would I hire the person who wrote this letter? If there is any doubt in your own mind, revisions are necessary. Finally, examine the tone of your letter to see if it sounds like you or a stereotyped example from reference books. There is no substitute for sincerity.

Advice from outsiders may make your letter more effective. This advice may come from placement directors, faculty advisers, personnel officers, employment agency counselors, or friends employed in the field you seek to enter.

Once a good letter of application has been developed, it may be used as a model, with slight revisions, many times. There is no valid excuse for a poor application letter. A good letter takes no longer to type and costs no more to mail than a poor one.

After you are satisfied with your letter, be sure to mail it at the most advantageous time. It should not arrive on a Monday, when the incoming mail is always heavy, or on a Friday, when the pressure of winding up weekly activities may prevent a thorough reading.

Send an application letter if you wish to avoid endless waiting in the lobby of a personnel office. It is always wise to have an appointment for an interview arranged by a good letter of application.

Exhibit 18   GEORGE JOHNSON'S LETTER

1712 Lanier Street
Macon, Georgia
May 1, 1962

President
University of Pensacola
Pensacola, Florida

Dear Sir:

As the spring quarter closes in June, the requirements for the master of arts degree in psychology will be completed at Normal State College, plus a few hours on my doctorate.

Professor Born, Chairman of the Psychology Department at Normal State, suggested that I contact you in regard to a teaching position for next year.

If no such vacancies exist, could my letter be forwarded or additional informational contacts sent to me?

Respectfully yours,

George Johnson

George Johnson

Exhibit 19 ANTHONY SPAULDING'S LETTER

1410 Euclid Avenue
Berkeley, California
March 15, 1962

Mr. Alfred Wolff
Personnel Director
Pacific Sales Company
978 Market Street
San Francisco 4, California

Dear Mr. Wolff:

Does your organization have an opening for a man with a good college activities record and a strong desire to make the field of sales his profession? If so, would you please consider this an application for a position with your company.

A June, 1962, graduate of the University of California, I am majoring in business administration. Included in this program of study were courses in marketing, sales analysis, sales management, business organization, statistics, accounting, and general economics. Through part-time sales experience in a hardware store I gained an appreciation of both people and basic sales techniques.

In addition to my studies I have participated in a number of activities which have helped me to understand better how to work with other people, as individuals and in groups. This year, I am a member of the Executive Committee of the Associated Students. As a member of Sigma Lambda Theta fraternity I have served as treasurer, social chairman, and vice-president. In this and other campus positions I have learned much about working with people. A summary of my qualifications is enclosed.

I am willing to work, to learn, and to take responsibility. I am not merely looking for a job. What I want is an opportunity: a chance to start at the bottom and advance on my own merits. May I have an interview at your convenience?

Very truly yours,

Anthony L. Spalding

Anthony L. Spaulding

Enclosure

Exhibit 20 JOHN YOUNG'S LETTER

1206 Forest Street
Kokomo, Indiana
January 17, 1962

Mr. Graham P. Fuller
Personnel Director
Midwestern Company
1900 Meridian Avenue
Indianapolis 8, Indiana

Dear Mr. Fuller:

Does the Midwestern Company have an opening for a man with a good knowledge of your company and the ambition to make sales his life's work? If so, would you please consider this an application for a sales position.

This application is submitted because two summers spent working in your Kokomo sales office demonstrated the quality of your products and your well-organized marketing program. Not only is each salesman permitted complete freedom to develop a sales program tailored to the unique needs of each customer, but every attempt is made to reward individual initiative in securing new customers.

Valuable background for your work should be furnished by a bachelor's degree in marketing to be awarded in June. You may also be interested in these additional college activities: Vice-President of the Independent Students' Association, Member of the Board of Directors of the University YMCA, and Treasurer of the Kokomo Chapter of the American Marketing Association. Exemption from military service is claimed through service in the U.S. Navy. You will find a resume enclosed.

The privilege of an interview, at your convenience, is requested.

Sincerely yours,

John W. Young

John W. Young

Enclosure

Exhibit 21   THEODORE PAGE'S LETTER

147 Green Street
Champaign, Illinois
January 4, 1962

Personnel Manager
Overseas Trading Company
400 Madison Avenue
New York 14, New York

Dear Sir:

Yes, this is a form letter. I think you will agree that any young man worth hiring should leave no stone unturned in his search for a career.

An American firm operating abroad, such as yours, may have difficulty finding men who will represent it overseas—and stay overseas. That is why you may want to know more about me.

I am married, a veteran, and a senior at the University of Illinois. In a month I will graduate with a degree in foreign trade. My wife and I are very seriously interested in living overseas, and we have had enough experience to know what we are getting into.

The experience and academic training which I can offer you cover the following fields: selling, accounting, international economics, and a reasonable knowledge of Spanish.

I do not expect to go abroad immediately, since there would be many things for me to learn first here in the States.

Salary, benefits, and comfort are of secondary importance to me. I am looking for a career that is challenging and interesting, and am confident of my ability to learn quickly and assume responsibility.

The enclosed data sheet should tell you many of the details about me. If you are interested in knowing more, I will be pleased to come for an interview. I look forward to hearing from you.

Sincerely yours,

Theodore L. Page

Theodore L. Page

Enc.

Step 2 LOCATE POTENTIAL EMPLOYERS

CHAPTER 7

RESEARCHING THE JOB MARKET

You are now ready for the biggest market research job of your life—locating the employer who best fits your requirements. Sound career planning and a good knowledge of the techniques of securing employment are effective only if your application is directed to the right employers. The next step in your job campaign is to compile a list of prospective employers.

HOW TO ORGANIZE YOUR RESEARCH

Proper organization and a systematic approach are important for this market research job. Start by developing a standard form for recording data on prospective employers. You may wish to start a notebook with a separate page for each employer or develop a set of contact cards (4- by 6-inch cards are recommended).

Whatever method you adopt, strive for uniformity and completeness in listing data. Thoroughness at this stage will save countless hours of repeating steps and adding information previously overlooked. Completeness will also facilitate the process of comparing employers later. As a minimum, you will want to include:

1. Name and address of the employer.
2. Telephone number (if readily available).
3. Name and title of personnel officer or proper person to contact.
4. Source of this lead.
5. Type of business, services, or products; size and function of governmental

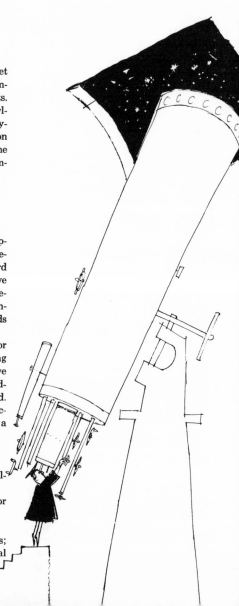

agency; or type of educational institution and curricula.

6. Notes on research reading or interviews (job nomenclature, training procedures, employer policies).
7. Other data (employees you know, community information, and similar facts).
8. Questions for future contacts.
9. Your contacts with the employer (telephone calls, letters, interviews). Date these so that you can quickly note your status and tell when an additional contact is advisable.

SPECIAL SOURCES FOR THE COLLEGE GRADUATE

A number of resource tools are specially prepared for the college graduate.

College Placement Annual (published annually by the College Placement Council, 35 East Elizabeth Street, Bethlehem, Pennsylvania). Contains an alphabetical listing and a brief description of over 1,800 organizations in the United States and Canada which regularly hire college graduates. This listing includes information on openings and gives the name, title, and address of the proper person to contact. It also contains helpful geographical and occupational indexes. Sponsored by the regional associations of college placement officers, it is distributed free through placement offices and through the U.S. Department of Defense.

College Placement Directory (published by the Industrial Research Service, Dover, New Hampshire, $12.50). Contains an alphabetical listing of over 1,500 employers, including name, location, type of business, name of personnel officer, and types of graduates sought. This book also has an occupational and geographical index. Many libraries or college placement offices have copies available.

Other publications are similar in function. Company information sheets (one-page sheets on employers) summarizing information on size, functions or products,

locations, types of graduates sought, and person to whom applications should be directed, are available through many college placement offices.

Foreign Operations (published by Foreign Operations, Inc., New Haven, Connecticut). Describes overseas employment opportunities in United States business organizations and governmental agencies.

Insurance World, 1957 (published by the Yale Daily News, Box 241, Yale Station, New Haven, Connecticut). Two booklets dealing with life insurance and property insurance. Describes the nature, scope, and functions or career opportunities.

Journal of College Placement (published quarterly by the College Placement Council, 35 East Elizabeth Street, Bethlehem, Pennsylvania, annual subscription, $5). Articles on career opportunities, employment techniques, and descriptive career ads from leading employers.

Wall Street 20th Century (published by the Yale Daily News, Box 241, Yale Station, New Haven, Connecticut). Sponsored by the Investment Association of New York. Describes career opportunities in the securities industry based on information originally developed by the *Yale Daily News.*

Career (published annually by Career, Inc., 15 West 45th Street, New York 36). Describes employment opportunities in approximately sixty organizations which have purchased space in this booklet. Distributed free on some campuses by student organizations or the placement office. Copies are also sold in retail stores. This same publisher produces *Careers for the Experienced Engineer and Scientist.* Advertisements are purchased by organizations seeking technical alumni.

EJD Job Directory (published by Decision, Inc., 2619 Colerain Avenue, Cincinnati 14, Ohio). Brief alphabetically arranged descriptions of 1,200 national companies, plus advertisements from the firms which pay for this publication. Distributed free to qualified technical personnel graduating in the last fifteen years. Available to others at $5.

STANDARD REFERENCE SOURCES

In addition to publications directed exclusively to the college graduate, a number of general standard reference sources are also available. These are useful in a variety of ways. An engineer, recently offered a position by a small firm at almost double his current salary, decided to check the financial standing of the firm. A poor rating influenced him to decline the offer. This was fortunate, as the firm went bankrupt a short time later.

Some of the more useful general references are noted here.

Moody's Manuals of Investment, 5 volumes (published by Moody's Investors Service, 99 Church Street, New York). Supplemented twice a week and revised annually. Provides financial descriptions, background information, and locations. Covers banks, insurance companies, and other financial agencies; municipals and governments; railroads; public utilities; and industrials. Available in the reference rooms of most larger libraries.

Poor's Register of Directors and Executives: United States and Canada (published annually by Standard and Poor's Corporation, 345 Hudson Street, New York 14). Alphabetical listing of approximately 27,500 leading business organizations, including address, principal products, number of employees, directors, and key officers. Found in reference rooms of larger libraries.

Thomas' Register of American Manufacturers, 5 volumes (published annually at 461 Eighth Avenue, New York 1). The first three volumes provide detailed information on leading manufacturing organizations by product, geographical location, and capital ratings. Volume IV is an alphabetical index. Volume V is a product index. Found in larger libraries, purchasing departments, etc.

Dun & Bradstreet (published at 99 Church Street, New York 8). Contains a geographically organized listing of approximately three million firms, including an evaluation of their financial responsibility and indication of type of business. No street addresses are given. Since it is a confidential credit reference, *Dun & Bradstreet* is available only to subscribers such as banks, financial institutions, and business firms.

Directory of American Firms Operating in Foreign Countries, by Juvenal L. Angel (published by the World Trade Academy Press, 50 East 42d Street, New York, 204 pp., $17.50). Lists approximately 3,500 American companies which operate in over fifty foreign countries. Listing is geographic, by countries, and alphabetical. Includes names and addresses of appropriate persons to contact in the United States. Available in some placement offices and libraries.

Trade Lists of American Firms, Subsidiaries, and Affiliates (published by the U.S. Department of Commerce, Bureau of Foreign Commerce, $2). Also available through field offices of the Department of Commerce. Lists, including addresses, of firms operating in approximately seventy foreign countries.

World Trade Directory Reports, prepared by the U.S. Foreign Service (published by the U.S. Department of Commerce, Bureau of Foreign Commerce, $1). Also available through field offices of the Department of Commerce. Contain basic commercial and financial information on foreign firms and individuals. Lists represent a consensus of reliable sources of information.

Chamber of commerce directories are published by most cities, some states, and many metropolitan areas and are available at cost, from 25 cents to $2.50. These directories usually list the major local industries alphabetically and by classification. Listings include address, telephone number, chief products, and the total number of persons employed. May be obtained through the chamber of commerce.

Classified sections of telephone directories are a useful source of names of prospective employers in a specific community.

Annual reports and financial analyses of stock corporations are often available from member firms of stock exchanges, from the firms themselves, or from libraries or placement offices. Inquiries should be addressed to the public relations department of the individual organization.

TRADE AND INDUSTRY REFERENCES

Literally hundreds of special directories list organizations in various fields. The lists are often as difficult to locate as they are valuable. Clues to the availability of lists may be found in these general publications, some of which should be in your library.

Public Affairs Information Service (published at 11 West 40th Street, New York). The bound annual publication of this service includes a list of publishers and trade and professional organizations. Particularly helpful is a section listing Directories of trade associations and professional societies.

Guide to American Directories (published biennially by B. Klein Company, 27 East 22d Street, New York 10). A guide to the availability of over 2,300 specialized lists in several hundred different fields.

Trade and Professional Association Members of the National Chamber (published by the U.S. Chamber of Commerce, 1615 H Street N.W., Washington 6, 132 pp.). A listing of associations of employers in various fields who are members of the chamber.

Sources of Business Information, by Edwin T. Coman, Jr. (published by Prentice-Hall, Inc., Englewood Cliffs, New Jersey, 1949). A multipurpose book including lists of available trade and professional directories, names and addresses of associations, and periodicals and books on subjects of business interest.

American Business Directories, by Marjorie V. Davis (published by the U.S. Department of Commerce in 1948). A roster of trade and professional associations and their addresses. This directory is now out of print.

The above books index hundreds of organizational and association rosters which may be helpful in your job campaign.

In addition, there are lists and directories dealing with specific fields. Typical examples are the following:

AM-FM Radio Station Directory (published by Television Digest, Triangle Publications, Inc., Box 700, Radnor, Pennsylvania).

American Library Association Membership Directory (published at 50 East Huron Drive, Chicago 11).

Association of Consulting Management Engineers Roster (published at 347 Madison Avenue, New York 17, 40 pp.).

Best's Insurance Reports (published by A. M. Best Company, Inc., 75 Fulton Street, New York 38). Analyses and descriptions of insurance companies.

Directory of Newspapers and Periodicals (published by N. W. Ayer & Son, West Washington Square, Philadelphia 6, 1581 pp.).

Education Directory, Part 2 (published annually by the U.S. Office of Education, 90 pp.). Available from the U.S. Government Printing Office, Washington 25. Lists county and city public and parochial school superintendents.

Education Directory, Part 3 (published annually by the U.S. Office of Education). Available from the U.S. Government Printing Office, Washington 25. Lists colleges and universities, including size, location, accreditation, and chief administrative officers.

Engineering Consultants Directory (published by the American Institute of Consulting Engineers, United Engineering

Center, United Nations Plaza, New York 17, 136 pp.).

House Magazine Directory (published by the Gebbie Press, 151 West 48th Street, New York 36, 457 pp.). A guide to over 4,000 house magazines.

Literary Market Place (published by R. R. Bowker Company, 62 West 45th Street, New York 36, 530 pp.). Contains seventy mailing lists indexing 10,000 people and firms in the publishing business.

Lovejoy's Prep School Guide (published by Harper & Brothers, 49 East 33d Street, New York 16, 120 pp.). Contains summaries of 1,800 private secondary schools.

McKittrick Directory of Advertisers (published at 840 Broadway, New York 3, 1800 pp.). Lists American and Canadian advertisers and 3,800 advertising agencies and their key personnel.

Mutual Savings Banks of the United States (published by the National Association of Mutual Savings Banks, 60 East 42d Street, New York 17, 200 pp.).

National Society of Public Accountants Membership Directory (published at 919 18th Street N.W., Washington 6, 87 pp.).

Personnel Blue Book (published by the American Academy of Personnel Executives, 927 15th Street N.W., Washington 5, 125 pp.). Lists personnel executives in approximately 1,800 companies.

Public Welfare Directory, by Loula Dunn (published by the American Public Welfare Association, 1313 East 60th Street, Chicago 37, 440 pp.).

Roster of Consumer Finance Companies (published by the National Consumer Finance Association, 1000 16th Street N.W., Washington 6, 189 pp.). Contains a detailed listing of 12,250 offices.

Security Dealers of North America (published by Standard and Poor's Corporation, 345 Hudson Street, New York 14, 1740 pp.).

Who's Who in Public Relations, by Robert L. Barbour (published by PR Publishing Company, Inc., Meridan, New Hampshire, 315 pp.).

Working Press of the Nation, 3 volumes, edited by Norman Seligman (published by the National Research Bureau, Directory Division, 415 North Dearborn Street, Chicago 10). The three volumes cover newspapers, magazines, and radio and television.

College faculty members or persons employed in your field of interest will often be able to provide lists of employment possibilities.

One final caution: Don't limit your search for potential employers to any single list, source, or booklet. You may find your future employer through a discussion with a friend or relative. Regardless of how you learn of potential employers, be certain to note the important data and study them carefully.

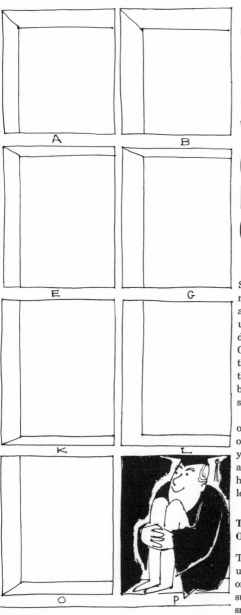

CHAPTER 8

WORKING EFFECTIVELY WITH YOUR COLLEGE PLACEMENT OFFICE

Some students dash into the college placement office around commencement time, apparently assuming that a job is picked up from the placement director as a diploma is obtained from the registrar. Others periodically wander in to see "if there are any good openings listed"; although never active enough to launch a bona fide job campaign, they are always shopping.

If you know how to take full advantage of its services, the placement office will be one of the most helpful organizations in your job campaign. No other agency has an interest in your vocational success and happiness comparable to that of your college placement office.

TYPES OF PLACEMENT ORGANIZATIONS

To obtain maximum assistance, you must understand how placement is organized on your campus. Some large institutions, such as Stanford University, and most small colleges have one centralized office handling placement for all graduates of the institution. In some schools the same office may be responsible for both vocational counseling and placement. On other campuses, each college or department develops its own program. The University of Illinois has twenty such decentralized placement offices. Still others separate offices by function. Indiana University has one office for business placement, a second for teaching. and a third for government. Many institutions have a separate office for teacher placement.

In colleges too small to have a formally organized placement program, assistance may be available through the office of the dean or the academic departments. Relatively few recruiters visit the small campus, however, and students will have to take the initiative in seeking out employers.

Some large institutions maintain off-campus placement centers for alumni. Cornell University maintains a New York City placement office. The University of Illinois has one in Chicago.

Not all college-based placement is professionally done. Until recently, for example, students at Lake Forest College operated the school's placement program. At the Harvard University Graduate School of Business, students organized a placement committee to supplement the regular office and to seek out opportunities in small businesses. Students share in the cost and leadership of the program and send a representative for the group to small organizations throughout the country.

SERVICES OF THE PLACEMENT OFFICE

The placement officer cannot hire you for a position, but in the role of *counselor* he can be a key person in your career planning. He is candidate-oriented, working with each graduate and many job openings, attempting to locate the best position for the candidate. By contrast, the employer's personnel officer is job-oriented, screening through many applicants to find the best one for the position. While a "good" placement is sound from the points of view of both the applicant and the employer, the placement officer's candidate orientation emphasizes his role in career counseling.

Your placement officer and members of his staff are usually the most readily available sources of information on the current labor market and specific employment opportunities. Their experience in helping prior graduates is available to you.

Your placement officer may help you to design your resume and letters of application and develop interviewing skill. He may refer you to successfully placed alumni or to contacts he has made through them. He may plan career conferences for student groups at which speakers in various fields discuss their occupations.

Many placement offices can help you to develop a background of information about your field and its employers through the help of materials contained in an occupational library. One of the best collections is the Career Reference Library developed by the Harvard University Office for Graduate and Career Plans (formerly the Office of Student Placement). This library illustrates the range of available materials. It is organized into the following sections: (1) books on careers; (2) directories of executives, manufacturers, and literary agencies; (3) folders (including annual reports and recruiting brochures) on 1,700 business and industrial firms; (4) a contact file of company recruiters and personnel directors; (5) information on the major governmental agencies; (6) information on the military services; (7) folders containing occupational information; (8) United States graduate study catalogues and fellowship directories and announcements; (9) foreign study catalogues and fellowship notebooks and directories; (10) subscriptions to leading business and placement magazines; and (11) classified telephone directories.

Campus interviews with prospective employers open up innumerable employment possibilities. During a recent year, the Columbia University Graduate School of Business had 80 employers recruiting accountants. University of Illinois elementary education majors were sought by 100 visiting school systems. Liberal arts graduates of Ohio Wesleyan chose interviews from among 250 different employers.

Such interviews permit a twenty- to thirty-minute exploratory talk with an employer definitely interested in hiring college graduates. These preliminary interviews take only a fraction of the time required to visit the employer at his place of business and involve no travel expense. Steele showed that the savings in travel costs to students who made initial employer contact through campus interviews ranged from $1,120 to $1,483 per senior.*

Although campus interviews are important, one large placement office estimates that only one-fourth of the employers with whom it works ever recruit on campus. Probably fewer than 10 per cent of the estimated 500,000 incorporated firms in the United States have ever conducted campus interviews. Smaller firms, organizations with only an occasional need for college men, and employers that prefer to hire experienced people ask for *direct referrals.* The resulting interviews take place in the employer's office. Normally, only a few candidates are nominated for each listing. This process of selective referrals is designed to save time for both the candidate and the employer.

Methods of handling direct listings vary. One placement office may mimeograph and distribute lists of currently available openings, while another may handle them in a highly confidential fashion, notifying candidates personally.

Your placement office may assist you through the *clerical aids* it provides. Some placement offices print individual data sheets or campus interview forms (Ex-

hibit 22) free of charge or at cost. These have been developed to save time for the student. They eliminate the necessity of filling out a different two- to eight-page application blank for each employer. At the same time they guarantee the employer basic data about each candidate. These forms are less flexible than the resume, although they may be filled with the materials which best support your career goals. If mutual interests develop, candidates then complete the employer's application blank.

Some offices collect references on candidates from faculty members, employers, and others and place these on permanent file. These references are confidential, never seen by the candidate, but available to prospective employers. Faculty references collected while you are a student are particularly helpful since they represent an appraisal made when you were best known and will always be available regardless of resignations or retirements.

Special credentials are prepared for teaching candidates. These consist of (1) copies of references, (2) personal history data (including employment), (3) summary of academic work, and (4) a statement of vocational or personal goals. Copies are sent to school superintendents or college deans, sometimes without the specific knowledge of the candidate. Many offices charge a nominal fee to cover the cost of developing such credentials.

The *alumnus* should start his job campaign with his placement office. Placement offices vary in policies and programs. However, most of them work actively with alumni seeking suitable positions. Many offices serve more alumni than graduating students. Strong alumni placement programs often characterize large urban universities, as more effective assistance may be provided to alumni within an area of convenient personal or telephone contact.

Alumni returning from military service usually find their college placement office the most convenient place to start their

* John E. Steele, "What Is Placement Worth?" *Journal of College Placement,* October, 1959, pp. 37-38.

Exhibit 22 CAMPUS INTERVIEW FORM

COLLEGE INTERVIEW FORM

(Please fill out neatly in ink and in own handwriting)

Photograph
(optional)

Name: Mr. ~~Mrs.~~ ~~Miss~~ PARKER / ROBERT / ALLEN

      Last Name   First Name   Middle Initial

Degree: B.S.   Major: E.E.   Minor or option COMPUTER

Graduation Date: JUNE, 1962

Present or College Address: 1479 EUCLID STREET, ORONO, MAINE

Permanent Address: 479 WHITE PLAINS ROAD, BRONXVILLE, N.Y.

College Phone: OR 2746   Home Phone: BR 7-2489

Personal Data: Height: 6'   Weight: 170   Single: ☒ Married: ☐   Number of Children _____

Date of Birth: JAN. 13, 1941 Place of Birth: NEW YORK, N.Y. Citizen of What Country: U.S.A.

Physical Limitations: NONE (HEALTH IS EXCELLENT)

Hobbies or Outside Interests: SKIING, FISHING, HI-FI, & CHESS

Father's Occupation (when active): TELEPHONE COMPANY EXECUTIVE

College and Community Information: Honors:

Professional Societies: I.R.E., A.I.E.E. (PROGRAM CHAIRMAN)

Activities: SUB-CHAIRMAN, WINTER CARNIVAL COMMITTEE
     MEMBER, STUDENT JUDICIAL COMMITTEE

Social Fraternity or Sorority: SIGMA CHI (VICE PRESIDENT)

Organizations Outside College: BOY SCOUTS OF AMERICA (ASSISTANT SCOUTMASTER)

Other Colleges or Universities Attended: (Give dates—degrees) COLBY COLLEGE (1958-1959)

Earned 40 % of total expenses while attending college. Grade Point Average 2.73 (A = 4; B = 3; C = 2)

Types of Work Desired: COMPUTER CIRCUITRY

Work Experience: Firm Name and Address	Type of Work	Full Time or Part Time	Dates Employed From	To
ELECTRICAL ENGINEERING DEPARTMENT UNIVERSITY OF MAINE	LABORATORY ASSISTANT	PART-TIME	9/61	5/62
RAYTHEON CORPORATION WALTHAM, MASS.	ENGINEERING TECHNICIAN	SUMMER	6/61	8/61
U.S. FOREST SERVICE, BRADDOCK NAT'L PARK, ME	FIRE FIGHTER	SUMMER	6/60	9/60
" " " " " " "	" "	SUMMER	6/59	8/59
GOOD HUMOR CORPORATION, WHITE PLAINS, N.Y.	ROUTE SALESMAN	SUMMER	6/58	8/58

Military Service Record: Present Draft or Reserve Classification: II-S

Military Service (if veteran): Dates: —   Branch: —

References: (List two faculty and two business—show name, title, employer, and address)

PROFESSOR J. C. SMITH	DEPT OF ELECT ENG	UNIV OF MAINE	ORONO, MAINE
PROFESSOR M. C. JOHNSON	DEPT OF MATHEMATICS	COLBY COLLEGE,	WATERVILLE MAINE
MR R. A. O'BRIEN	SENIOR ENGINEER	RAYTHEON CORP	WALTHAM, MASS.
MR M. V. GOODMAN	SALES MANAGER	EASTERN RADIO CO,	YONKERS, N.Y.

Date Available for Employment: JUNE 20, 1962   Today's Date: MARCH 1, 1962

search for employment. Younger alumni are permitted by some offices to participate in available campus interviews. Some offices refuse to help a graduate unless he has given his current position at least a two-year trial.

Programs of placement offices and the current demand for college graduates present a unique problem to graduating students. Instead of learning the techniques of a well-balanced employment campaign (searching out prospective employers, preparing the resume, and developing the letter of application), many of today's graduates obtain their first position as the result of a half-dozen interviews easily scheduled on the campus. There is a tendency to depend too much on the placement office.

Failure to master the technique of securing employment may prove a handicap in subsequent job changes.

HOW TO RECEIVE MAXIMUM ASSISTANCE FROM YOUR PLACEMENT OFFICE

You should make initial contact with the placement office no later than the beginning of your final semester or next to last quarter. Candidates for advanced degrees should register at the start of their final year. Interviews for Ph.D. candidates are often conducted a year or two before graduation. If you register early, you will probably receive more attention.

Most offices require a registration inter-

Exhibit 23   WHAT YOU SHOULD KNOW ABOUT YOUR PLACEMENT OFFICE

What is registration procedure?
What forms must be completed?
Is there a charge? How much?
When should you see your placement officer?
With whom will you be working? His function?

Are credentials or data sheets prepared?
When is background material for them due?
Are faculty or outside references collected?
Is an application photograph required?

How are campus interviews publicized?
Where can you obtain material on recruiting organizations?
How are interviews arranged?

How are direct job listings publicized?
How are contacts made?

Is there an occupational library?
What does it include?

What services are available to alumni?
Are fees charged for alumni services?

view with a staff member. If it is optional, take it. A favorable comment from a placement officer acquainted with their qualifications has helped thousands of graduates land jobs. In this initial contact candidates and placement officers have an opportunity to develop a mutual understanding which should make subsequent contacts more profitable.

To guarantee that you will receive maximum assistance from the placement office, you should thoroughly understand its policies and procedures. At the Office of University Placement of Columbia University, for example, fall interviewing is limited to Ph.D. candidates and midyear graduates at the master's level. Exhibit 23 summarizes what you should know about your placement office.

It is the candidate's responsibility to keep in close touch with his placement office. To complete your obligation to the placement office, report carefully and promptly your offers, your problems, and your acceptance of a position. This is proper courtesy in view of the assistance which you have received. Many alumni filing for replacement have been chagrined to discover that they failed to report their first position.

A growing number of schools are offering *courses* in occupational adjustment, job-seeking techniques, or career opportunities in professional fields. These courses are often taught by members of the placement staff or operated in conjunction with the placement program. Most of these courses are offered for credit, usually one hour.

They seek to help the student with his occupational adjustment after college in the same way that freshman orientation courses aid adjustment to college.

One course of this type is Placement and Personal Adjustment to Business, offered by the School of Business at the University of Arkansas. The Placement Office of Southern Illinois University sponsors a course entitled Job Orientation. Business Careers is a two-quarter hour course offered by Ball State Teachers College. Northeastern University offers three courses in the field of job placement catering to the special needs of engineering, business administration, and liberal arts students. The Dean of the College of Business Administration of Long Island University conducts a course labeled Executive Leadership.

Some placement offices have developed a series of meetings on job-seeking techniques called "senior seminars." Others provide lectures on vocational adjustment or on various occupations. The formal courses, as well as the series of meetings, generally cover such topics as taking an inventory of one's interests and qualifications, selecting a vocational goal, making up resumes, writing application letters, developing or utilizing sources of prospective employers, preparing for the interview, following up on job prospects, and adjusting to the job and employer after graduation. In addition, such courses and meetings provide a thorough opportunity to explain the operations, policies, and procedures of the school's placement service.

CHAPTER **9**

OTHER ORGANIZATIONS THAT MAY HELP YOU

A discouraged alumnus sat across the desk from a college placement officer. He had been seeking work for four months and had become very discouraged about his job campaign. He enumerated his unproductive application letters and listed his fruitless calls on employers.

It took only a few minutes to diagnose a part of his problem. He was handicapping himself by using only a 50 per cent job campaign. To supplement his own efforts he should have enlisted the support of outside agencies.

PRIVATE EMPLOYMENT AGENCIES

Fee-charging employment agencies may be particularly helpful when you are moving into a new geographical area in which your own contacts are weak. They have local contacts and a practical knowledge of employment conditions. Selecting an agency in Poughkeepsie, Laramie, or Tacoma presents no problem. Only a handful work with professional candidates. However, large cities such as Boston, Chicago, or Los Angeles have several hundred. Look for an active agency; it will offer more choice. The more applicants it has, the more listings it has. Newspaper advertisements and size of staff are rough indications. Locate agencies which specialize in your field. One may concentrate on advertising and public relations, another on engineering and science, and a third on accounting, banking, and insurance. You can learn about specialization by studying advertisements. You may find helpful information on New York agencies in the free guide published by the *New York Times*.

Look for accreditation. Commercial agencies often belong to professional associations. Many of the better teacher placement agencies belong to the National Association of Teachers' Agencies, 82 St. Paul Street, Rochester 4, New York. Agency personnel often belong to the American Institute for Employment Counseling; individuals may qualify as Certified Employment Counselor or Registered Employment Counselor. Membership information is available through the American Institute for Employment Counseling, 19 Pine Avenue, Long Beach 2, California.

Do not hesitate to ask for this kind of information and, if you have doubts, check with the local chamber of commerce or better business bureau.

Finally, study an agency critically from your personal standpoint. Does it provide the service you need? Are you receiving personal attention? Does the interviewer understand your problems and interests? Most employment agency interviewers are quick in action and frank. Candidates must expect this kind of assistance rather than the long-range career approach of the college placement officer. Remember that agencies receive their income from placements only, so naturally they will be aggressive in seeking jobs for you. This has both advantages and disadvantages. Some agencies will register only those people whom they feel can be quickly placed. In order to make an easy placement, unscrupulous agencies may refer good candidates to inferior positions where they will obviously please the employer. Accept referrals only to positions which appear to fit your plans.

The employment agency week begins ostentatiously, with large display ads in the classified sections of the Sunday newspapers. Avoid the Monday morning crowds. There are normally just as many good jobs and less competition later in the week. Check agency interviewing hours. Some agencies close their doors for part of the day to solicit new openings and contact candidates.

In addition to completing the agency's application form, you will be asked to sign a statement guaranteeing to pay a commission for any position accepted through its referral. This commission is usually between 5 and 10 per cent of the first year's salary. Although employers sometimes offer to pay the agency's commission in areas where good candidates are hard to find, the candidate often assumes legal responsibility for the commission if the employer does not pay. You also agree not to share job leads with others. You should honor this obligation.

A typical agency contract is shown in Exhibit 24.

An example of a leading teacher placement agency is the combined American College Bureau and the Fisk-Yates Teachers Bureau. Located in Chicago, this agency has specialized for over seventy years in the teacher placement field. Its American College Bureau concentrates on placement of college and university faculty, librarians, deans, and other administrators. The Fisk-Yates Teachers Bureau specializes in public and private school positions, both teaching and administrative. Candidates register by mail or in person. There is an annual $2 registration fee. If a position is accepted, candidates pay an additional commission of 5 per cent of the first year's salary.

If used intelligently, private employment agencies may save you a lot of time and play a helpful role in your job campaign.

STATE EMPLOYMENT OFFICES

These offices are taking an increasing interest in professional, managerial, and scientific placement. Employment specialists in these areas have been added in some offices and a central information bureau has been developed with the announced purpose of placing specialized candidates in high-level positions. The over 1,800 state employment offices are located in medium-sized and large cities. In addition to placement activities, they provide vocational testing, counseling, and labor market information. All their services are free to both applicant and employer.

Exhibit 24 TYPICAL EMPLOYMENT AGENCY CONTRACT

I accept your offer of employment assistance on the following conditions:

1. For any position accepted through your services, I agree to pay a commission based upon the scale established by state law. I note this scale ranges from 25% of the first month's salary for positions paying under $225 per month up to 60% for positions paying over $400.

2. For positions accepted within the Continental United States, the commission must be paid within three paydays or six weeks, whichever period is shorter.

3. If the total commission is paid within ten days from date of employment, the above fees are reduced 10%.

4. If I accept a position and subsequently decide not to report for work, I agree to pay one-quarter of the normal commission.

5. If the position is terminated by the employer, my liability is limited to 10% of my total earnings.

6. I agree to treat confidentially employment information received from your agency and not to share this information with other persons.

7. I will not reveal to my present employer the fact that your agency accepted my voluntary application.

Signature: _____

Date: _____

Social Security Number: _____

A strong state employment office is the Professional Placement Center of the New York State Employment Service in New York City at 444 Madison Avenue. Here a staff of over 100 works with 6,000 applicants a month. In addition, members of various professional associations act as consultants on professional developments and employment problems in specialized fields. Publications of the center include *From Campus to Career,* which analyzes employment possibilities open to liberal arts graduates in various fields, and *Guide to Preparing a Resume.*

Not all state employment offices have such high standards. Many spend much of their time handling subprofessional openings. Other offices administer unemployment compensation claims, and this further dilutes their energies.

EXECUTIVE RECRUITING FIRMS

In the past two decades, executive recruiting firms have assumed an increasingly important role in filling many of America's best jobs. Because they deal almost exclusively with top-level jobs and their work is highly confidential, it is difficult to learn about them. Often they are vaguely described as "management consulting firms." While some such firms have executive search departments, many restrict themselves to analyzing an employer's problems and suggesting solutions. Executive recruiting (or "search") firms are engaged by organizations with management vacancies to conduct an extensive search for the best candidates with the right background and abilities, at the appropriate salary level, and with at least an interest in learning more about the opening.

Often it is difficult to distinguish between an executive recruiting firm and a private employment agency. Both may use the names of principal partners as their name. Some agencies misleadingly describe themselves as consultants. Major differences exist. Search firms work on a national basis. Private agencies are local. Search firms deal with high-level positions and assume more responsibility for filling positions. (By New York State law, executive recruiting firms may not handle jobs with an annual salary of $9,000 or less, as these vacancies are considered more appropriate for private employment agencies.)

Edmund G. Hergenrather of Hergenrather Associates estimates that his firm fills 70 to 80 per cent of the executive requirements received from employers. Search firms work closely with the hiring organization, frequently conducting an extensive on-the-spot analysis of a position before starting recruitment.

Because of the confidential way in which executive recruiting firms operate, some candidates who might have been interested in a position will never hear about it. On the other hand, many graduates not actively seeking another position will be contacted by executive search firms trying to fill vacancies. This confidential procedure is in direct contrast to the procedure of employment agencies, which usually advertise their listings both to attract suitable candidates for current openings and to build up their files of active registrants to fill future listings.

Sound advice on how to make the best use of recruiting firms is given by Samuel H. Beach of the New York City firm of Beach and Hunt, Inc. Beach was formerly director of placement at Columbia University. He emphasizes five points for the effective use of recruiting firms in an employment campaign.

1. Make sure that you are in the right age and salary bracket to benefit from executive recruiting firms; otherwise, you may be wasting time. Eight out of ten positions filled by executive search firms are for men in their forties. Most positions are at an annual salary of at least $15,000.

2. Feel free to call your qualifications to the attention of executive recruiting

firms. Most of them maintain extensive files of potential candidates for new positions. These files include information on candidates who have contacted them as well as names gleaned from conversations with top executives, from newspaper or magazine clippings, and from a variety of other sources. These files are indexed for ready reference. When a position is listed with an executive recruiting firm, its application files are first screened for nominees. This is then supplemented by a confidential, but aggressive, search for additional qualified candidates from outside sources.

3. Share your availability with a number of executive recruiting firms. Most top-level positions are listed with only a single search firm. There is no clearinghouse between firms. To ensure that your qualifications will be reviewed by an executive recruiting firm, you must check with it personally.

4. Make your initial contact with an executive recruiting firm by mail. Many men feel incorrectly that they must have a personal appointment to receive help from an executive recruiting firm. Most search firms hear from scores of candidates each week and couldn't begin to see them all personally. The chief interest of the executive recruiting firm is to ascertain your qualifications, index them, and hold them on file for review as appropriate vacancies are listed.

You are normally better off conducting a mail-order campaign instead of contacting search firms personally, as your goal is to place your qualifications before as many of these firms as possible.

In preparing a resume for a search firm, include full details on your background, vocational interests, current salary and total compensation, and the actual names of your employers. Be sure to point out your accomplishments

and other evidence of your ability to get results. Normally you have little to fear about your availability being discovered by your current employer, as executive recruiting firms are known for their confidential handling of employment information.

5. Be wary of executive recruiting firms which charge money for their services. Some firms will summarize your qualifications, add their own evaluation of your potential, and share this record with potential employers. These firms charge a flat fee ranging from $200 to $1,000, but with no guarantee of success. Employers often react negatively to this approach. They take the evaluative comments from the hired search firm at less than their face value and wonder why the candidate didn't prepare his own presentation or make direct contact himself.

Should you be contacted by an executive search firm for a possible opportunity, don't expect to talk directly to the employer involved, at least not at first. In addition to an extensive written application, the search firm may invite you for a series of interviews and may ask you to take a battery of tests. Face-to-face contact with the prospective employer may not materialize until the executive search firm is convinced that you possess most of the qualifications required for the opening. The entire process could easily take several months; therefore, this source has limitations for the applicant who is forced by circumstances to obtain another position immediately.

Lists of reputable firms may be obtained from several organizations: the American Management Association, 1515 Broadway, New York 36; the Association of Consulting Management Engineers, Inc., 347 Madison Avenue, New York 17; and the Association of Executive Recruiting Consultants, Inc., 60 East 42d Street, New York 17.

PROFESSIONAL ORGANIZATIONS AND PUBLICATIONS

Many professional societies and associations provide organized placement assistance. Even the least active organizations help through contacts at conventions. Two groups with well-developed programs are the American Chemical Society and the American Economic Association.

Members of the American Chemical Society receive employment assistance on both the national and local levels. The national staff of the ACS includes a placement specialist who coordinates placement activities, prepares articles on employment for publication, and, in general, funnels employment interest into productive channels. During its national meetings, the ACS operates the National Employment Clearing House. Between meetings, it maintains a Regional Employment Clearing House in its offices in New York, Chicago, and Washington. Here ACS members seeking positions may leave copies of their resume for review by employers.

The society's *Chemical and Engineering News* lists professional opportunities and situations wanted advertisements. Unemployed members of the Society are allowed free "situations wanted" advertisements in three issues of the *News* each year.

Locally, many of the larger sections play an active role, collecting candidates' papers for examination by employers, maintaining a file of job opportunities, or publishing a list of openings. Some enlist experienced chemists for job consultation.

The American Economic Association holds an annual midwinter meeting and forms the backbone for the annual meetings of the Allied Social Science Associations. This group includes also the American Statistical Association, the American Marketing Association, the American Finance Association, the Academy of Management, the Industrial Relations Research Association, and the American Association of University Teachers of Insurance.

The AEA's convention placement service helps candidates interview representatives of business and industrial organizations, government agencies, and colleges or universities. Applicants may send resumes ahead of time to simplify interview arrangements. The American Economic Association's *American Economic Review* regularly summarizes openings and carries digests of applicants' qualifications. These programs are typical of the employment interest of professional groups.

The *Accounting Review,* the official publication of the American Accounting Association, carries job summaries in practically all issues through its "Placement Exchange."

The American Personnel and Guidance Association publishes an extensive employment bulletin six or eight times a year listing openings and summarizing qualifications of candidates. The association also maintains files of candidates and openings in the student personnel field at its national headquarters in Washington. During its annual spring convention, the association's placement center is used by 400 to 500 candidates and approximately 300 employers.

The American Marketing Association maintains two placement services. One is for academic positions and is operated by a committee of professors of marketing who circulate information to college marketing departments. The second service circulates information about nonacademic jobs and candidates through a special publication entitled *The Market Place.* As is true of many professional groups, candidates must be members of the American Marketing Association to take advantage of these services.

One caution is important. Membership in a professional association may be helpful from an employment standpoint and certainly is desirable as a source of contact in your field. The chief value of professional associations comes, however, from development of a better understanding of your field, acquaintanceship with its leaders, the opportunity to keep up with latest developments, and the chance to develop your own professional reputation.

The young graduating student has the advantages of campus interviews, close contact with his college placement office, and general skills. The experienced candidate, by contrast, must take full advantage of all employment resources, as few opportunities may exist for his specialized job requirements. Fortunately, the agencies described in this chapter are available to help the graduate, but they can help only if he takes the initiative in making contact.

Step 3   CONTACT PROSPECTIVE EMPLOYERS

CHAPTER 10

HOW TO APPLY FOR A JOB

The Army uses a training film to depict the importance of selecting the right weapon for each problem faced by the soldier. The film shows the infantryman when to use the rifle, bayonet, or hand grenade and when to call for tank support, artillery fire, or air assistance. For persons engaged in job campaigns the most powerful "weapons" (resume, letter of application, etc.) are effective only if directed to the right person, at the right time, and through the right method.

The usual methods of contacting employers include campus interviews, direct employer contacts, want ads in newspapers and professional publications, and civil service examinations.

CAMPUS INTERVIEWS

If you are now a college student, campus interviews usually represent the most efficient way to begin your job campaign. Campus interviews are as effective as they are convenient. One placement office recently reported that 85 per cent of the engineering seniors, 70 per cent of the business administration seniors, and 45 per cent of the liberal arts seniors secured their first positions through campus interviews.

Keith Duffin, the director of placement for Brigham Young University and former president of the College Placement Council, estimates that over 1,500,000 individual interviews are scheduled on college campuses each year.

DIRECT EMPLOYER CONTACTS

Despite the growth of campus interviews, the initial employment contact for many graduates will occur in the employer's office. The most effective appointments are those which are prearranged.

The written letter of application and the resume remain the preferred method of contact. Employers find it easier and more efficient to study and evaluate qualifications before replying. Many personnel officers refer mail applications to heads of operating departments for review before deciding on an interview.

Under some circumstances, the initial contact may be by telephone. Graduates who have been referred by an employment service for a particular opening in their community should usually schedule an appointment by telephone. Candidates for positions involving considerable use of the telephone may call to demonstrate their abilities. Telephone contacts usually settle immediately the question of employer interest. The employer may ask the questions which are of greatest interest to him. Telephone contacts permit some salesmanship on the part of the applicant, but it must be tactful.

"Cold turkey" calls on employers are rarely effective. Many employers are available only by appointment. However, candidates occasionally find employers who prefer to see unannounced candidates on the theory that they "have initiative."

Normally, initial contact should be made through the employer's personnel office; this is why it exists. Furthermore, personnel office files contain the most complete source of employment information. Applications for positions on a major policy-making level or for positions which may have to be specially created may be addressed to the president or top operating managers.

Idealistic college graduates often are uncertain about the proper role of friends and relatives in approaching employers. They often receive conflicting advice. The keynoter at a recent college career conference shocked his audience by stating that the best way to get a job was described on the door of the auditorium: "Pull." You may occasionally use friends to arrange employment appointments, but any offer must result from your qualifications—not your acquaintances.

WANT ADS IN NEWSPAPERS AND PROFESSIONAL PUBLICATIONS

Want ads may be helpful in at least two ways. They may help you find a job or at least may provide useful background information on the current job market—openings, qualifications, and salary levels.

Reading help-wanted ads Want ads have significant characteristics. They are usually directed toward the specialist who has established skills and can fill an immediate need. The volume of newspaper ads is far heavier on Sunday, on the assumption that Sunday papers are read more thoroughly. Come-hither phrases such as "promotion guaranteed," "big future," or "rapid advancement" often attempt to build up poor opportunities.

Employment advertisements in metropolitan dailies are usually arranged for ready reference. The typical classification system is:

> Help Wanted—Agencies—Female
> Help Wanted—Female
> Help Wanted—Agencies—Male
> Help Wanted—Male
> Situations Wanted—Female
> Situations Wanted—Male

There are two types of want ads. Straight listings (Exhibit 25) include both a description of the position and the name of the employing organization. From the candidate's standpoint, straight listings are the most helpful. Knowing the position and the organization, he will investigate only situations which appear to fit his job plans. Blind listings (Exhibit 26) do not indicate the name of the employer and often omit the type of business and job title. Replies are usually directed to a box number. Employers use blind ads to restrict applications to mail, avoid the necessity for acknowledging or interviewing unqualified applicants, and keep recruitment confidential.

Some blind ads state, "Our own employees have been notified of this opening." This assures the employed candidate that he will not be embarrassed by applying to his current employer.

Before replying, analyze an ad to discover what the employer *must* have and what he *prefers* to have. Your reply must cover listed or suggested specifications.

Keen competition exists for the better-advertised positions. Candidates must expect to reply to many advertisements without arousing any significant employer interest. Many candidates respond carelessly to an advertised position, using a general form or a mimeographed letter. This is a mistake—any position worth investigating deserves your best effort.

You may be asked to apply by telephone for some positions—particularly sales positions. Treat telephone replies as seriously as written applications. Before dialing, review your qualifications and the most effective method of presenting them.

A New York City life insurance salesman with an annual income of over $60,000 builds many of his largest sales on telephone solicitations. He uses a standard and carefully developed sales presentation. You may not be able to earn $60,000 a year with your telephone, but you can improve your chances of landing a job by planning your conversation before dialing.

Writing situation—wanted ads Employers read situations-wanted ads (Exhibit 27) when they seek a particular set of qualifications. Want ads should be used only when you are ready to accept a position immediately. These principles should

help you to write more effective advertisements:

Be positive. Avoid words such as "inexperienced," "beginner," or "unskilled."

Note order of listings. Are advertisements listed on a first-come, first-listed basis? Or are they arranged alphabetically? If advertisements are listed alphabetically, you may wish to write your ad so that it will be one of the first. For example, "Accountant" will precede "Head Accountant" and follow "Able Head Accountant."

For larger publications with well-defined classifications, you may prefer to begin your ad with an accurate and concise description of the position sought, such as "Computer Programmer" or "Fashion Coordinator."

Strive for the unusual. Only a unique advertisement stands out. A Chicago employment agency called attention to its

Exhibit 25 HELP WANTED AD, STRAIGHT LISTING

EDITORIAL ASSISTANT

Female college graduate sought for general duties with a new magazine. Age to 30. Newspaper or magazine experience helpful. Do not apply in person. Send complete resume to Southern Living, 1042 Peachtree Street.

Exhibit 26 HELP WANTED AD, BLIND LISTING

TRAINING OPPORTUNITY WITH SUBCONTRACTOR

Unlimited growth prospects for a young, ambitious man with college background. Send full details. Box 29. Glen Rock, N.J.

listings by announcing "Business jobs for philosophy majors." Obviously, these positions were open to any liberal arts or business graduate. While you should avoid misleading phrases, your ad should attract favorable attention.

Consider the most effective length. One study showed that less than 5 per cent of all want ads were over six lines long. You may wish to use one long ad rather than several of typical length.

Emphasize what the employer wants. "Research Director" as the title of an ad brought no response. An ad labeled "Lacquer Chemist" by the same man attracted seven replies and a position as chief chemist in a research laboratory.

Consider a third-person approach. An ad placed for you by someone else (Exhibit 28) may attract favorable attention.

Select the right media. Trade journals

Exhibit 27 FIRST-PERSON APPROACH TO A SITUATION-WANTED AD

PURCHASING AGENT

Ten years' experience electro-mechanical components, castings, plastics, glass, ferrous and nonferrous metals. Excellent administrative, cost reduction background. Contact Box 183.

Exhibit 28 THIRD-PERSON APPROACH TO A SITUATION-WANTED AD

President of Corporation

Wishes to place industrial advertising manager whose position is being abolished through merger with another organization. Candidate is experienced and successful in developing a multimedia program. College graduate with strong civic and professional interests. Contact Box 369.

may be more helpful than regular newspapers. Finance candidates may advertise most effectively in the *Wall Street Journal*. Publishing aspirants may use *Publishers' Weekly*.

Respond to all inquiries. As a matter of courtesy, reply to all employers who answer your ad. This helps the employer keep his files straight. At some future date, he may even have a more attractive opportunity. If he is favorably impressed with your businesslike approach, he may even share your availability with other employers.

CIVIL SERVICE EXAMINATIONS

Some graduates fail to apply for positions with governmental agencies because they are confused by civil service hiring procedures. Information about civil service positions is readily available from printed announcements which present title of opening, duties, employing agency, educational and vocational requirements, salary range, instructions for applying, and deadline for submitting application. Some announcements publicize general recruiting programs, such as the state of Minnesota Social Worker examination, the U.S. Civil Service Commission's Accountant and Auditor Examination, or the Potomac River Naval Command's Scientist and Engineer examination. Other announcements concern specific openings for which recruiting is conducted only as vacancies occur, such as Dade County, Florida, recruiting a Personnel Director, or the State of Illinois an Employment Interviewer III.

The most important examination to graduating students is the Federal Service Entrance Examination (FSEE), which is offered several times a year to recruit candidates in fields other than engineering and science. It channels graduates into over sixty major career fields. A more difficult option within this examination selects graduates for management intern positions.

Exhibit 29 REGIONAL OFFICES OF THE UNITED STATES CIVIL SERVICE COMMISSION

First Region: Post Office and Courthouse Building, Boston 9, Mass.

Second Region: News Building, 220 East 42d Street, New York 17, N.Y.

Third Region: Customhouse, Second and Chestnut Streets, Philadelphia 6, Pa.

Fifth* Region: Peachtree-Baker Building, 275 Peachtree Street, N.E., Atlanta 3, Ga.

Seventh Region: Main Post Office Building, 433 West Van Buren Street, Chicago 7, Ill.

Eighth Region: 1114 Commerce Street, Dallas 2, Tex.

Ninth Region: New Federal Building, 1114 Market Street, Saint Louis 1, Mo.

Tenth Region: Building 41, Denver Federal Center, Denver, Colo.

Eleventh Region: Federal Office Building, First Avenue and Madison Street, Seattle 4, Wash.

Twelfth Region: Appraisers Building, 630 Sansome Street, San Francisco 11, Calif.

* There is no fourth or sixth regional office.

Federal announcements are displayed most conveniently in post offices. State and municipal openings are posted in public offices. Most college placement offices collect current civil service announcements. Directories describing governmental agencies and the positions for which they normally recruit are published by some state and municipal civil service organizations and by many civil service regional offices. The regional offices are located in major cities (Exhibit 29).

Most governmental positions are filled through a formal examination. Three types of examinations are used in most civil service systems; they may be used singly or in combination.

The first type is the standard written examination. The typical civil service examination is a written multiple choice test (Exhibit 30) designed to measure one or more of the following: intelligence, aptitude, or knowledge. The Federal Service Entrance Examination is an example. Nor-

Exhibit 30 TYPICAL QUESTIONS FROM WRITTEN CIVIL SERVICE EXAMINATIONS

(A) VOCABULARY QUESTIONS

Veracity means
the same as   (1) vital   (2) misleading   (3) valid
        (4) falsehood   (5) truth

Affluent means
the same as   (1) engaged   (2) rich   (3) afraid
        (4) fixed   (5) not fluid

(B) CUBE COUNTING

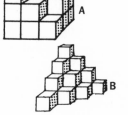

Figure **A** contains _____ cubes
(1) 24   (2) 22   (3) 27
(4) 16   (5) none of these

Figure **B** contains _____ cubes
(1) 12   (2) 20   (3) 10
(4) 16   (5) none of these

(C) ARITHMETIC PROBLEMS

Three timers are set to ring every 4, 5, and 6 minutes respectively. If all three ring simultaneously, how many minutes will it be before all three ring simultaneously again?

(1) 20   (2) 24   (3) 30   (4) 60   (5) 120

What one number can replace both question marks?

$$2:? = ?:32$$

(1) 4   (2) 16   (3) 8   (4) 12   (5) none of these

mally, written tests are based on a maximum of 100 with a passing score of 70.

Oral examinations, when used, are a secondary screening device, used with applicants who have passed the written examination. They are given to candidates for career positions as foreign service officers by the U.S. Department of State and to prospective management interns for assignment with government agencies in Washington.

Unassembled examinations are a third type. Eligibility for appointment is based upon an evaluation of the candidate's training and experience as shown in an application and other written evidence of

Exhibit 31 VETERANS' PREFERENCE IN CIVIL SERVICE EXAMINATIONS

	EARNED SCORE	VETERANS' PREFERENCE	TOTAL SCORE
Veteran	85	5	90
Disabled veteran	75	10	85
Nonveteran	83	0	83

qualifications. No formal test is administered. This procedure is often used to expedite hiring when a shortage of qualified candidates exists. Governmental research organizations usually hire scientists through an unassembled examination.

The names of successful candidates are placed on a civil service register. A register ranks candidates in order of their total scores. Veterans often have priority, with particular preference given to a disabled veteran (Exhibit 31). In some situations, a disabled veteran is automatically placed at the top of a register.

Each civil service system operates under its own unique rules. There are typical procedures. Periodically, an inquiry of availability may be sent to persons on a register to determine whether or not they are currently interested in employment. Failure to respond may be taken as an indication of no interest, and the candidate may be dropped from the register.

When an opening occurs, three or more persons at the top of the register are called for interviews. Final approval is given by the employing agency, which usually must hire one of these three or leave its opening unfilled, unless the position is filled by promotion or transfer. Some civil service systems, however, permit an employing agency a wider choice among the highly qualified candidates.

Registers may be used until depleted, but more frequently they are replaced automatically after one year by a new examination and a new register. The open continuous examination inserts the newly eligible candidates in an existing register and permits a recently successful and top-rank candidate to be certified ahead of persons in lower rank, irrespective of their dates of qualification.

Personal visits and demonstrations of interest in an agency may make the difference between no position and an appointment. There are extraroutine ways in which an application may be expedited. For example, an agency may request papers of a candidate "within reach" on a register—especially a register such as the FSEE, which is used by many agencies. An agency also may ask for selective lists from general registers of eligible persons with particularly appropriate backgrounds. Occasionally, an agency may have authority to hire on a temporary appointment anyone who has passed the required examination, rather than having to consider the top names on the register. Such temporary appointments may become permanent.

Regardless of the method used to contact employers—whether through a campus interview, by writing a letter of application, or as a result of qualifying through a civil service examination—you are now ready for the key phase of the employment process, the interview.

CHAPTER 11

CONDUCTING THE EMPLOYMENT INTERVIEW

The interview is the climax of your job campaign. It is a two-way exchange of information between an employer and a job candidate to discover whether mutual interest exists. The interview is not a form of third degree. Most personnel interviewers are pleasant and helpful. They represent organizations which are public relations–minded.

The employment interview has three main objectives: to help the employer obtain information not included on the resume or application blank, to enable the applicant to obtain information not covered in the employer's written materials, and to establish a bridge of contact between the organization and the prospective employee.

PREPARATION

Competition for preferred jobs is very keen. A ratio of 10 to 20 applicants interviewed for every 1 hired is normal. A leading advertising agency reported that it interviewed 1,400 college graduates in a twelve-month period. From this group, it selected 5 copywriters and 75 "general-development" people to start in the mail room and work up.

A large metals-producing company interviews approximately 600 professional-level applicants a month and normally hires only 30.

According to a survey reported in September, 1961, by the Midwest College

Placement Association, firms employ only 4.8 per cent of college graduates interviewed for technical positions (engineering and scientific) and only 5.6 per cent of candidates interviewed for nontechnical positions.

Sound preparation not only helps you to know what to say during the interview, but also builds up your confidence and helps you sell your services more effectively. A good salesman spends hours developing his most effective sales approach and couples his technique with a thorough knowledge of his product.

J. Douglas Snider, director of the Bureau of Personnel Relations and Placement of Indiana University, makes these suggestions on preparation for the interview:

1. Be familiar with the employer's history, products or services, and principal locations.
2. Be prepared to explain your interest in the employer.
3. Be ready to ask at least two good questions concerning the employing organization, its products or services, or its policies. These should not be questions that are readily answered in the employer's literature.

It is important that questions be based on accurate information. A recruiter for a petroleum company recently commented that on one campus, where seniors had obviously been instructed to ask questions during the interview, many of the student questions were about products the company didn't manufacture and plants the company didn't own.

An excellent summary of tips for the interview appears in the booklet *Your Job Interview* by Robert P. Stieglitz, distributed free by the College Relations Department of the New York Life Insurance Company, 51 Madison Avenue, New York. Copies may be obtained through many college placement offices.

Students review before an examination;

job candidates should review before an interview. As Snider suggests, review your personal inventory and be able to summarize your qualifications.

1. Study your personal inventory so that you are in a position to know and sell your product—yourself.
2. Be prepared to tell in two minutes your potentialities for service with the employer.
3. Be sure to bring a resume or portfolio to the interview.
4. Carry a pen and note paper.
5. Use the interviewer's name and know his function in his organization.
6. Practice a firm handshake.
7. Dispose of chewing gum and lighted cigarettes before entering the interviewer's office.
8. Be sure to arrive at the place of the interview five minutes early.

Dress in conservative good taste (Exhibit 32). Remember that your grooming expresses your attitude toward yourself, which is bound to affect the interviewer's attitude toward you.

THE INTERVIEW ITSELF

The interview begins the moment you arrive at the employer's office. The reception room is not a lounge area or a dating bureau. Be courteous, cooperative, and dignified because an adverse comment from a receptionist or secretary has hurt many job candidates.

If you are normal, you will be nervous as you approach the interview. Fortunately, a touch of nervousness is an asset—it helps to keep you alert and enthusiastic during the interview.

Greet the interviewer by his name. (Don't be so naïve as to call the interviewer by his first name merely because he uses yours or because he introduces himself as "William Brown" rather than "Mr. Brown.")

Follow the cues given by the interviewer. Shake his hand if he offers it. Women should take the initiative if they wish to shake hands.

Pause a moment before taking a seat, both to provide an opportunity for the employer to offer you a seat and for him to indicate where he would like you to sit. Smoke only if invited or after asking if you may. If there is no ashtray in sight, take the hint. Scrupulously avoid reading anything on the interviewer's desk—the reasons are obvious.

Interviewers encourage conversation by asking questions about your background. They are frustrated by candidates who respond laconically with "Yes" or "No." Even more frustrating are candidates who talk too much and without pausing. Employers wish to participate in the conversation and to direct it into areas of particular interest.

The interview is the optimum moment for presenting job qualifications. Too many candidates write dynamic letters of application or prepare beautifully organized resumes but don't use the interview to bring out their qualifications.

Flexibility is a must in interviewing. For example, just as an interviewer asked a candidate to tell his qualifications, he was interrupted by a telephone call. What should the candidate have done at the end of the conversation? Reply to the question or wait for the interviewer to restate it? He might say "In response to your question just before the phone rang. . . . " A candidate for a management position found that, instead of having a private conversation with the personnel director, he was

Exhibit 32 GOOD GROOMING FOR THE INTERVIEW

MEN	WOMEN
Wear a clean, pressed and conservative suit with a clean white shirt.	Wear a simple suit or dress.
Wear a conservative necktie.	Use conservative high heels; no novelty items here.
Wear plain socks and shined shoes.	Wear conservative nail polish and lipstick.
Avoid gaudy or flashy rings.	Have a neat hair-do; ballroom coiffures are out.
Have your hair neat and trim; long hair, ducktails, and sideburns are out.	Leave flashy earrings in your jewelry box.
Clean and trim your fingernails.	Be moderate in use of perfume.

escorted into a large room to be interviewed by a dozen executives. The self-confidence that comes from good preparation is the only protection against such unexpected developments.

Hints for interviews include also the following:

1. Forget about politics, religion, and similar areas of individual opinion. If discussion arises on these subjects, have the courage to state your convictions—and provide logical evidence to support your views.
2. Be positive in your comments. One man obtained a keenly sought-after job because he spoke so enthusiastically about his school. His positive attitude made a deep impression on the employer.
3. Employers are not interested in your "troubles." They wish to hire only people who can manage their own affairs effectively.

WHAT THE EMPLOYER LOOKS FOR

Interviewers usually want to cover such specifics as interest in the work involved. Does the position satisfy the candidate's basic needs and interests? Some employers try to gauge a candidate's vocational interests by asking a sales candidate, "Have you considered personnel work? It seems that you are particularly well qualified for this field." The candidate with firm interests will refute the question and indicate why he selected the field of sales.

Personality—physical appearance and vigor, self-confidence, sense of humor, ability to converse, poise, and friendliness—all are important to an employer.

He is interested in scholarship. Immediately after four years of college, the best criterion of your performance is your scholastic record.

He wants to know about your activities. Participation in extracurricular programs and the particular activities selected provide helpful clues regarding your leadership potential.

Work experience is significant. The kind of work experience, how much the student contributed to the cost of his education, and the initiative shown in obtaining jobs indicate whether the applicant has learned to work under and with others.

He checks on special aptitudes and skills. The candidate's aptitudes and the requirements of the job should be harmonious.

Frank S. Endicott, director of placement at Northwestern University, has surveyed employers to find the questions most frequently asked during employment interviews. The questions, listed in Exhibit 33, provide a helpful check list for interview preparation.

Women are frequently asked how long they intend to work. They should realize that employers need to estimate how much training they can afford to give and therefore need to know whether a candidate is engaged, planning to work for five years, or presently free from any personal involvement.

Most of the larger organizations have a structured rating scale which is used by interviewers to evaluate applicants. A typical interview rating sheet is shown in Exhibit 34.

WHAT YOU SHOULD LOOK FOR

Preoccupation with answering the employer's questions makes candidates forget that the interview is a two-way process. They should be just as interested in learning about the situation as employers are interested in evaluating them. Avoid the "show-me-what-you-have-to-offer" attitude, however. Through the interview, the candidate should learn about the training offered, the function of the position, its future, and the quality of the organization.

In a national survey to ascertain what college graduates seek in a position, the Opinion Research Corporation discovered

Exhibit 33 QUESTIONS MOST FREQUENTLY ASKED BY EMPLOYERS DURING INTERVIEWS

1. What are your future vocational plans?
2. How do you spend your spare time? What are your hobbies?
3. In what type of position are you most interested?
4. Why do you think you might like to work for our company?
5. What courses did you like best? Least? Why?
6. Why did you choose your particular field of work?
7. What percentage of your college expenses did you earn? How?
8. How did you spend your vacations while in school?
9. What do you know about our company?
10. What qualifications do you have that make you feel that you will be successful in your field?
11. What are your ideas of salary?
12. How do you feel about your family?
13. If you were starting college all over again, what courses would you take?
14. Do you have a girl? (or a boy friend?) Is it serious?
15. How much money do you hope to earn at age thirty? thirty-five?
16. Do you think that your extracurricular activities were worth the time you devoted to them? Why?
17. Why do you think you would like this particular type of job?
18. Tell me about your home life during the time you were growing up.
19. Are you looking for a permanent or temporary job?
20. Do you prefer working with others or by yourself?
21. What kind of a boss do you prefer?
22. Are you primarily interested in making money or do you feel that service to your fellow men is a satisfactory accomplishment?
23. Do you live with your parents? Which of your parents has had the most profound influence on you?
24. How did previous employers treat you?
25. What have you learned from some of the jobs you have held?
26. Have you ever changed your major field of interest while in college? Why?
27. Do you feel you have done the best scholastic work of which you are capable?
28. Have you ever had any difficulty getting along with fellow students and faculty?
29. Which of your college years was the most difficult?
30. Do you like routine work?
31. What is your major weakness?
32. Do you demand attention?

33. Are you willing to go where a company sends you?
34. What job in our company would you choose if you were entirely free to do so?
35. Is it an effort for you to be tolerant of persons with a background and interests different from your own?
36. What types of people seem to "rub you the wrong way"?
37. Would you prefer a large or a small company? Why?
38. What are the disadvantages of your chosen field?
39. What have you done that shows initiative and willingness to work?

---

that college graduates rated most highly chances for advancement and interesting work. Far down on the scale came salary, benefits, and recreational activities (Exhibit 35).

THE SALARY QUESTION

Most authorities agree that initial salary is relatively unimportant. Ed Smith of the Armstrong Cork Company says: "Look for future opportunity, not initial salary. Your starting salary is only a temporary one. You will eventually be paid as much as you are worth. Too much interest in salary may hurt your career chances."

A good rule of thumb is to concentrate on the job first and salary second. Your bargaining power on salary is obviously better after the employer has decided that you are his choice. You should, however, know the customary salaries for college graduates with your background and experience. Most larger organizations have a definite salary range for each position. Normally, the personnel man must offer a salary falling within the range authorized for the position under discussion. The usual practice is to start new employees at the bottom of the range to permit future salary increases (Exhibit 36).

If you are asked point blank about salary, a good response may be "Salary is important, but secondary to opportunity. I would like to discuss the future in the position rather than its beginning salary."

Study salary offers carefully so that you will know what they mean. If you are expected to travel, who pays the expenses? What deductions are taken from your salary? Is any of your income exempt from taxes? Will you encounter many expenses which you must pay for yourself?

Your employment counselor should know current salary levels for persons with your training as well as in your geographical area.

TERMINATING THE INTERVIEW

Candidates should be sensitive to signs that the interview has run its course. Campus interviews are usually scheduled for twenty or thirty minutes, but employment interviews with potential supervisors or managers will generally take forty-five minutes or longer. Some blunt officials will terminate an interview by standing up, holding out their hand, and thanking you for coming in. Most employer representatives, however, expect you to sense the proper time to leave.

Important steps in terminating the interview are the following:

1. Thank the interviewer for taking time to talk with you. You should not apologize for "taking his time."
2. If you can do it sincerely, tell him that you are interested in the position and that you would appreciate being considered. Many candidates mistakenly

Exhibit 34 INTERVIEW RATING SHEET USED BY EMPLOYER

Date _____

Professional Interview Report

Fill out immediately after each interview and return to
Employment Supervisor with application and qualification record

Name of Candidate _____ School _____

Degree _____ Field _____ Grad. Date _____ Place of Interview _____

Appraisal

	Exceptional	Excellent	Acceptable	Fair	Poor
General First Impression					
Personal Appearance					
Physical Appearance					
Initiative in Conversation					
Ability to Express Himself					
Potentialities					
Final Impression					

(Check appropriate characteristics)

Personality			*Poise and Manner*	*Maturity*
_____ Dominant	_____ Quiet	_____ Excellent	_____ Alert	_____ Unusual
_____ Strong	_____ Affable	_____ Good	_____ Overbearing	_____ Advanced
_____ Average	_____ Friendly	_____ Pleasing	_____ Confident	_____ Normal
_____ Passive	_____ Breezy	_____ Poor	_____ Ordinary	_____ Insufficient
_____ Negative	_____ Naive	_____ Timid	_____ Nervous	
			_____ Awkward	

If this individual were qualified in your field, would you like to have him work for you?
_____ Like very much; _____ Would like; _____ Would accept; _____ Prefer not to have.
Logical Assignments (1)_____ (2)_____ and (3)_____
In competition with our professional staff, what would you estimate the evaluation of this
individual to be after 5 to 10 years in our employ?   A   B   C   D   (circle one)

Amplifying Comments:

_____
Interviewer

Exhibit 35 HOW COLLEGE MEN RATE FOURTEEN FACTORS BEARING ON JOB CHOICE

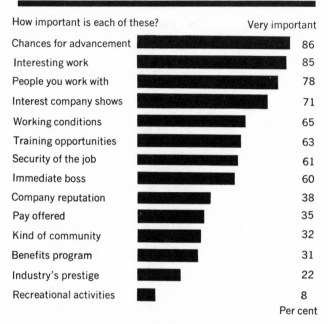

How important is each of these?   Very important

Chances for advancement	86
Interesting work	85
People you work with	78
Interest company shows	71
Working conditions	65
Training opportunities	63
Security of the job	61
Immediate boss	60
Company reputation	38
Pay offered	35
Kind of community	32
Benefits program	31
Industry's prestige	22
Recreational activities	8

Per cent

Source: "How Companies Can Improve Their College Recruiting Programs," Opinion Research Corporation, Princeton, N.J., December, 1954.

assume that employers sense their interest.

3. Know the next steps to be taken on your application. Will the employer contact you? Should you come back for testing? Does the interviewer expect you to think over the position and let him know if you are interested?

4. Leave promptly when you are through. Lingering departures are no more ef-fective in the interview situation than in social life.

5. On the way out, briefly thank the receptionist or person who introduced you.

As soon as possible after the interview, write down what you have learned. Don't trust your memory to keep employers and jobs straight. You may also wish to include questions for subsequent contacts.

Exhibit 36   TWO TYPICAL STARTING-SALARY PLANS FOR COLLEGE GRADUATES

Most plans are based upon a fixed monthly minimum with additional increments depending upon the qualifications of individual candidates.

EMPLOYER A's SALARY PLAN

Base Salary: X dollars

Experience Factor
  $15 for each year's experience prior to obtaining bachelor's degree
  $25 for each year's experience after receiving bachelor's degree

Personal Factor
  $10 for an above average candidate
  $25 for an exceptional candidate
  $40 for an outstanding candidate

EMPLOYER B's SALARY PLAN

Base Salary: X dollars

Experience Factor
  $15 for each year's work experience

Military Service Factor
  $15 for completion of military service
  $25 for military service pertinent to position sought

Dependent Factor
  $15 for wife
  $10 for one or more children

Step 4   FOLLOW UP EMPLOYMENT PROSPECTS

CHAPTER 12

EMPLOYER VISITS

Employer visits are trips to plants, offices, laboratories, stores, or schools by candidates whose qualifications have been previously screened. They are now an established part of the recruitment process. They usually precede the actual job offer. In some cases, candidates initially interviewed at an employer's place of business may be recalled for a more intensive contact.

The first contact between a candidate and an employing organization is often made by a representative whose jurisdiction is limited to initial screening. The decision to hire, which follows an employer visit, is usually the responsibility of the supervisor involved.

A study by the Opinion Research Corporation involving a selected group of college seniors showed that 64 per cent of the group had been on an employer visit.* They felt that these aspects were emphasized during their visits: (1) specific job opportunities—what new people do, where they work and with whom; (2) company operations—products and processes; (3) working conditions in the plant and living conditions in the community; and (4) quality and background of company personnel.

Not all employers provide the opportunity for a visit prior to a job offer. Government agencies, educational institutions, and many commercial businesses may not offer employer visits—or not paid visits. Many employers are unable to invite job candidates from distant parts of the coun-

* How to Recruit the College Men You Want, Opinion Research Corporation, Princeton, N.J., December, 1954, p. 31.

try. Statistically, most persons invited for employer visits receive job offers. Because of their cost, employers limit invitations to candidates with strong qualifications.

WHEN TO MAKE EMPLOYER VISITS

Visits should usually be deferred until most of your employer contacts have been made. Obviously, these visits immediately precede job offers—if one is to be made. It would be unwise to visit Company A when the initial interview with Company B will not occur for several weeks or months.

Employer visits are limited by several considerations. The most obvious is the sincerity of your interest in an organization. The statement of the *Principles and Practices of College Recruiting* which appears in the Appendix, says that a candidate should accept an invitation for a visit "only when he is sincerely interested in exploring employment with that employer." Another limitation is that of time. Graduating students are too busy during their last few months of college to take unnecessary trips.

The usual visit is concluded within a single eight-hour work day. Candidates usually have some freedom in selection of the date. Astute candidates often schedule employer visits during school vacations. A Monday or Friday date is often preferred to permit travel over weekends.

Allow some leeway in employer visitation arrangements in case your visit is extended at the employer's request or you encounter travel difficulties. A graduating civil engineer decided to visit five employers on successive days. His Monday and Tuesday visits in La Crosse and Milwaukee, Wisconsin, worked out very well. However, bad weather canceled his Tuesday evening airplane flight to Indianapolis, and he spent most of the night on trains and buses to arrive in time for his Wednesday morning appointment. Faced with another airplane cancellation Wednesday evening, he spent a grim night traveling to Pittsburgh. What had been planned as another pleasant airplane flight Thursday evening from Pittsburgh to Lancaster, Pennsylvania, turned out to be another long ride on a local train. The first two employers offered positions, the last three did not.

EXPENSE ACCOUNTS

Don't assume that all organizations will pay expenses. If the invitation is not clear, your placement officer may know the employer's policy. Otherwise, you should not hesitate to ask the employer.

Take along plenty of money on employer visits. Travel changes may cost money and you will need some working capital. A few employers send a travel advance along with their invitation. Others pay total estimated expenses during the visit itself, with a later adjustment possible. Most employers reimburse for expenses only after the visit, and from one to four weeks after receiving your itemized travel costs.

A senior at a large eastern university recently bragged about his unique method of raising money. He accepted invitations to visit three employers in the same city. Instead of prorating his expenses among these organizations, he charged each employer the complete travel costs from his home! His action violated accepted ethics, and seriously risked his own professional reputation.

Employers frequently check with each other. Overlapping expense accounts could easily be discovered. More important is the question of ethics. A candidate with a sincere interest in his career will recognize the vital importance of developing a reputation for integrity.

During a meeting of the Midwest College Placement Association, the question was asked: Do you know of an actual case in which a job candidate falsified an employer visit expense account? In a group of about five hundred personnel officers and college placement directors, only four could report actual instances of cheating.

The best way to protect your reputation is to keep accurate records of your expenses. If you are driving, note the speedometer reading at the beginning and the end of your trip, deducting mileage incurred en route for any personal business. Ask for the appropriate allowance for mileage. Hotel bills, airplane or train ticket stubs or copies should be included with your itemized expense list as supporting evidence. If you visit several employers on the same trip, ask for suggestions on how to prorate your expenses so that each employer will assume his proper share of the cost of your trip.

WHAT TO EXPECT

Look for multiple interviews with top executives, heads of operating divisions, your prospective supervisor, and a representative of the personnel department. Some employers use multiple interviews on the theory that a person cannot successfully play a role if he is faced with the grueling challenge of an entire day of interviews. In an attempt to see candidates when they are relaxed, one personnel director drives them to the airport at the end of their visit.

Employers may test the sincerity or conviction of candidates by presenting a discouraging picture of the position, its working conditions, or its training assignments. An example is the sales supervisor who exaggerates the amount of required travel to make sure that the candidates will not object to the travel actually required.

Other employers make the applicant sell himself. One executive purposely says little during the interview on the theory that if you can keep a person talking for ten minutes without interruption, you will be able to measure his true personality.

A sales candidate was handed a box of the employer's product and told to reenter the room and sell this to the interviewer.

When the candidate returned, the employer shouted, "I'm too busy to talk to you. Get out of here." Fortunately, few visits involve such a rigorous test.

Don't expect to meet the representative with whom you talked before. One major firm uses 500 men in its initial recruiting program, but only a few participate in employer visitation programs.

Some typical employer visit programs are described in Exhibit 37.

TESTS AND PSYCHOLOGISTS

An employer visit is a logical time to expect psychological tests and, in some cases, a psychological examination. This is the employer's last chance to measure your suitability.

Many employers develop their own battery of tests. The battery of tests used by the Atlantic Refining Company includes a mental alertness (intelligence) test, an interest test, a temperament test, a supervisory practices test, and a mechanical aptitude test (for engineering candidates only). The tests are used in an exploratory way to discover clues which should be investigated further through depth interviews or weak points which should be remedied during the training period.

The validity of psychological tests may be limited by the fact that candidates are taking them not to learn more about themselves, but to pass an employment hurdle. (In fact, employers usually refuse to give candidates the results of the tests which they have taken.) The most obvious example occurs in response to interest and personality test items. Take for example, the question: "How would you most like to spend an evening? (a) reading a book, (b) conversing with a small group of close friends, or (c) attending a party at a service club." Obviously, the "best" answer to this question might be different for an applicant seeking a position selling life insurance, an applicant applying for admission to a theological seminary, or an

Exhibit 37 TYPICAL EMPLOYER VISIT PROGRAMS

COLLINS RADIO CORPORATION

"In addition to the usual interviews and a plant tour, Collins includes an informal technical quiz during the applicant's visit. The quiz is conducted by a member of the engineering management staff and measures the candidate's knowledge of his major field and his approach to the solution of technical problems. A Collins spokesman says that candidate response is good; most invited candidates consider this test a sound approach to hiring."

SEARS, ROEBUCK AND COMPANY

"Visitation programs vary from one section of the country to another. Candidates are assumed to have a fundamental knowledge of retailing. If the applicant desires more first-hand information, he is encouraged to visit stores and talk with the personnel manager and with trainees, but no formal arrangements are made for these visits. Candidates are asked to take a battery of psychological tests designed to supplement the knowledge gained through the interview."

PROCTER & GAMBLE COMPANY

"As a part of its philosophy under which much of the firm's recruiting is a paramount responsibility of each major function of the business, candidates for positions with Procter & Gamble will visit a P&G installation offering the type of work in which they are interested. In many cases, these plants or offices represent the place where successful candidates may begin their careers. Depending upon the field of interest, applicants may also expect from fifty to ninety minutes of psychological tests."

SCOTT PAPER COMPANY

"Candidates for sales positions with Scott usually spend a full eight-hour day accompanying an experienced salesman on his rounds. This demonstrates how company policies are translated into everyday actions and permits direct observation of the working conditions and the physical and mental strains of the job."

MARSHALL FIELD AND COMPANY

"To supplement and personalize its interviewing and store tour program, Marshall Field attempts to arrange a private luncheon for each candidate with a current employee. Whenever possible, candidates lunch with a recently employed college graduate from their own school."

MARATHON CORPORATION

"Candidates are invited for visits in groups of around a dozen, all interested in the same type of work (sales, accounting, production, etc.) As outlined by Alan MacGregor ('Promotion from Within,' Journal of College Placement, December, 1956, pp. 94-96), the group usually assembles around 2 p.m. on Sunday. The men spend the rest of the day (a) being photographed, to aid in personalized identification; (b) receiving orientation briefing; (c) taking a battery of tests; (d) participating in a question and answer period about opportunities in the company; (e) touring the community to view its residential, commercial, and recreational facilities; and (f) dining with many of the men who will interview them during their visit.

"The next day, each man is interviewed by six to eight company representatives. Between interviews, the men are encouraged to talk with Marathon employees and to tour the plants and offices. At the end of the day, the candidates are thanked for coming, bid good-bye and informed that they will receive an offer or a rejection within twenty-four hours.

"The Marathon interviewers then assemble, each having ranked the candidates from 1 to 12. These ratings are consolidated and test results and other information correlated. A decision is made on each candidate and individual telegrams are sent the next morning conveying this decision."

---

applicant filing for an editorial position.

An entertaining chapter entitled "How to Cheat on Personality Tests" appears in *The Organization Man.** These clues are provided for answering items on personality tests.

When in doubt, however, there are two general rules you can follow:

1. When asked for word associations or comments about the world, give the most conventional, run-of-the-mill, pedestrian answer possible.
2. To settle on the most beneficial answer to any question, repeat to yourself:
    a. I loved my father and my mother, but my father a bit more.

*William H. Whyte, Jr., *The Organization Man,* Simon and Schuster, Inc., New York, 1956, pp. 405-410.

b. I like things pretty much the way they are.
c. I never worry much about anything.
d. I don't care for books or music much.
e. I love my wife and children.
f. I don't let them get in the way of company work.

Despite their limitations, psychological tests play an important role in sound employee selection. Any attempt to distort the results may work to your disadvantage. There is no point in landing a job if you will be unable to perform its duties properly or if you will be unsuited for it temperamentally.

No preparation is required for psychological tests. A cardinal rule for success is to work rapidly and accurately on tests which have a time limit, as both factors affect your final score.

The psychologist is playing an increasingly important role in both initial selection and screening for specialized assignments or promotion. Dean Witter and Company, a West Coast stock exchange member, realizes that it takes more than college education, ambition, and salesmanship to make a good stock broker. Dean Witter supplements standard interviews and tests with an interview conducted by a psychologist. The expense of this interview is more than repaid by a careful selection of candidates for a training course that costs more than $10,000 per man.

An interview with a psychologist is a vital part of the procedures used by the National Aluminate Corporation of Chicago in hiring sales candidates. The interviews, which last half a day, are conducted by a psychologist familiar with National Aluminate's special job requirements. (Incidentally, the company has ignored the psychologist's "don't-hire" recommendation only three times. Each time negative personality factors developed which eventually forced the company to release the men involved.)

Most employers do not use psychologists in hiring men at the entry level. However, should you encounter a psychologist, remember that his goal is the same as yours: to ensure placement of the right person in the right job. Therefore, be yourself rather than what you think he wants you to be.

CHAPTER 13

MAKING YOUR EMPLOYMENT DECISION

Every week candidates with "job-offer" problems come into placement offices. Some report, "I accepted a position with School B, but now School A has offered a much better position. What should I do?" Others say, "Several employers seem interested, but none has contacted me since the initial interview." A final group worries about "which job offer to accept."

This final phase of the employment process requires patience, for employer decisions are usually slower than anticipated; optimism, to avoid the handicap of appearing too anxious for a position; and good judgment, to handle successfully a number of different and unique employers.

You will find the process of following up job leads much simpler and more effective if you have developed a form of some sort for recording the progress of your job campaign. For example, you may wish to devise an employer control record (Exhibit 38) on which to jot down your follow-up procedures with various prospective employers so that you can see at a glance what your next steps in each case should be.

FOLLOWING UP JOB PROSPECTS

Alert candidates follow up prospects to remind the employer of their availability, highlight their interest in his organization, and encourage more serious consideration of their candidacy. Employers often wonder about applicants who have an interview, seem genuinely interested and quali-

	NAME OF EMPLOYER	Barton & Sons	Service Instruments Co.	Acme Manufacturing Co.	E.T. Foote + Sons	Carver Corp.	Yarnell & Co	Meredith Corporation	Smith & Johnson Co.	Luther Manufacturing Corp.
	Inquiry or application letter	3/15	3/9	3/7	3/2	2/27	2/2	2/26	2/20	2/20
	No answer								3/20	
	No possibilities			3/17						3/6
	Application submitted	3/24	3/17		3/13	3/6	3/10	2/28		
	No current opening									
	Interview offered	4/6	3/24		3/20	3/8	3/15	3/7		
	First interview	4/9	4/4		3/29	3/19	3/20	3/9		
FOLLOW-UP ACTION	Letter		4/15			3/19	4/1			
FOLLOW-UP ACTION	Telephone call	4/18	4/25			4/10		3/11		
FOLLOW-UP ACTION	Personal visit					4/20				
	Second interview						4/6			
	Later interviews									
EMPLOYER ACTION	Rejection		4/25			4/25		3/16		
EMPLOYER ACTION	Stalled									
EMPLOYER ACTION	Job offer	4/20			4/5		4/10			
YOUR ACTION	Rejected offer	4/28			4/12					
YOUR ACTION	Stalled						4/17			
YOUR ACTION	Accepted						4/28			

fied for a position, and then make no further contact.

Avoid an air of impatience. The impatient applicant may antagonize the employer by pressing for a decision he is not ready to make.

A more intelligent job decision may be made if offers, or rejections, arrive at the same time. Following up on employers who are slow to respond may encourage a decision and permit you to choose from the greatest number of job alternatives.

Follow-up contacts should usually include (1) self-identification, including background (school attending or current employment, etc.); (2) a "job handle" for the position desired; (3) summary of past contacts with the employer, such as interviews, letters and employer's response; (4) an inquiry regarding the status of the opening; and (5) an offer to provide additional information. A variety of approaches are available.

Letters are the most common follow-up method. They remind the employer of your interest without the interruption caused by a telephone call or personal visit. A follow-up letter may summarize your most pertinent qualifications or share additional assets. A formula for a follow-up letter is given in Exhibit 39.

A telephone call is the quickest and preferred method for local contacts. The employer may conveniently ask questions or arrange for another appointment. A telephone follow-up should be brief, such as "Mr. Johnson, I am Frank Crawford whom you interviewed for your sales position on April 24. I am calling to remind you of my interest in your opening. Am I still being considered? Would you care for additional information?"

A personal visit should be avoided unless you normally have some face-to-face contact with the potential employer. The amenities involved in ushering you in and out of an office make visits time-consuming and are usually no more effective than a telephone call.

Placement officers or employment counselors may be asked to check on the status of an opening. Employers often talk more frankly to a third party. This approach has some disadvantages, as the employer may wonder why you did not personally follow up your previous contact. This technique should be reserved for the climax of your job hunt.

How often should follow-up contacts be made? No fixed rule is possible. Follow the instructions given during your initial interview. Normally, contacts should be no more frequent than once every ten days or two weeks. More frequent contacts become necessary with the emergence of a job offer and the need to collect all available information before making a decision.

HANDLING SEVERAL OFFERS SIMULTANEOUSLY

The college graduate with a successful job campaign will have to choose from among several job offers. Selection of the right position is complicated if offers are received prior to a decision on a position of particular interest.

There are several helpful principles to follow in handling offers:

1. All job offers should be acknowledged immediately. The employer may not expect an immediate decision, but he would appreciate knowing that you received his offer. Unless you tell him, an employer has no way of knowing whether you are considering or ignoring his offer.

2. When you reply, indicate when you expect to make a decision. Sometimes an employer suggests a time limit which he considers reasonable. If you must delay, request a general rather than a specific time extension. "A few days" provides more leeway than "until Thursday."

3. If you are obviously not interested in a position or have more attractive

Exhibit 39   FORMULA FOR A FOLLOW-UP LETTER

514 North Clark Street
Springfield, Massachusetts
May 20, 1962

Mr. John U. Arthur
Chief Auditor
Northeastern Company
45 West Broad Street
Boston 12, Massachusetts

Dear Mr. Arthur:

First paragraph: Thank him for the interview and express appreciation for the courtesy or consideration extended to you. Remind him of the position for which you were interviewed and the date and place of the interview.

Second paragraph: Reaffirm your interest in the position and organization. Mention anything you have done since the interview which demonstrates your interest in the opening (i.e., additional research on the employer, conversations with local representatives, etc.).

Third paragraph: Submit any information you wish to add to your application. Express willingness to provide additional data, if requested.

Final paragraph: Close with a suggestion for further action, such as your availability for additional interviews at the employer's convenience.

Very truly yours,

Samuel R. Beane

Samuel R. Beane

offers, withdraw your application. This simplifies matters for both you and the employer.

4. If a decision is required on an attractive offer, don't hesitate to contact other employers of interest. A straightforward approach is usually the best. Tell the employer that you have another offer but are interested in his organization and wonder about the status of your application. Most employers will frankly share your status, indicate when a decision may be made, or expedite matters to encourage a speedy decision. Psychologically, there is value in demonstrating to an employer that while other employment opportunities exist you are still interested in him.

EVALUATING OFFERS

A position may be selected on the basis of your personal feelings toward an employing organization, its policies, its employees, and your sense of identification with the organization. There is a definite need, however, for a more scientific approach to the selection of your career employer. The Radio Corporation of America (Exhibit 40) suggests that graduates investigate the type of work, opportunity for advancement, company reputation, provisions of training program, salary, job security and employee benefits, and educational opportunities, among other aspects of the job.

Several mathematical formulas have been developed for evaluating career offers. An excellent *Comparator* for business and industrial offers is the one developed by Elwood G. Glass, Jr., Manager of Recruitment for the Standard Oil Company of Ohio.

The formula evaluates initial training, supervision, working conditions and facilities, the employer, the field, advancement, benefits, expenses paid, advice of others, compensation, the job and geographical location. Using a 0 to 3 value scale, the

Exhibit 40 WHAT TO INVESTIGATE ABOUT A POTENTIAL EMPLOYER

1. Type of work
2. Opportunity for advancement
3. Company reputation
4. Provisions of training program
5. Salary
6. Type of industry
7. Facilities
8. Educational opportunities
9. Job security
10. Employee benefits
11. Cost of living in company location

candidate rates each factor on its importance to him. 0 indicated "no importance whatsoever"; 1 is "of slight importance"; 2 is "important"; and 3 is "very important" (Exhibit 41).

The factor "prestige of job" may be considered very important by one candidate who weights this category 3. A candidate who considers this irrelevant marks it 0. Using a separate column for each potential employer, the candidate ranks (not rates) each employer on each item. The lowest ranking indicates the least desirable situation. For example, "prestige of job" may be contrasted among four employers. If the position with Employer C offers the least prestige, the rank would be 1. If Employer A offers the next least prestige, the rank would be 2, etc.

The rankings for each employer are then multiplied by the value assigned to each item. This gives the total score on each factor for each employer. For example, if "prestige of job" is assigned a value-scale rating of 3, and if Employer B has a relative rank of 3, the total score for Employer B would be 9 (3×3). Employer C, with a relative rank of 1, would earn only 3.

The employer with the highest score should prove the most desirable for you. Relative differences in scores indicate

Exhibit 41 COMPARATOR FOR BUSINESS AND INDUSTRIAL OFFERS

	VALUE SCALE	EMPLOYER A		EMPLOYER B		EMPLOYER C		EMPLOYER D	
INITIAL TRAINING									
Planned training	2	3	6	2	4	4	8	1	2
Type of training	3	1	3	3	9	4	12	2	6
Scope of training	3	1	3	3	9	4	12	2	6
Subtotal			12		22		32		14
SUPERVISION									
Personality of supervisors	1	1	1	4	4	2	2	3	3
Their ability to train me	3	1	3	4	12	3	9	2	6
Subtotal			4		16		11		9
WORKING CONDITIONS AND FACILITIES									
Offices and laboratories	1	2	2	3	3	4	4	1	1
Equipment	3	1	3	3	9	4	12	2	6
Associates	3	4	12	2	6	3	9	1	3
Nonprofessional assistance	2	2	4	4	8	3	6	1	2
Geographical location(s)	3	1	3	3	9	2	6	4	12
Subtotal			24		35		37		24
THE EMPLOYER									
Prestige of job, reputation	3	2	6	3	9	4	12	1	3
Size	1	4	4	3	3	1	1	2	2
Growth potential	3	3	9	4	12	2	6	1	3
Stability	2	1	2	3	6	4	8	2	4
Diversification	2	3	6	2	4	4	8	1	2
Personnel policies, general	2	3	6	4	8	2	4	1	2
Ratio of professional employees to total	1	—	—	—	—	—	—	—	—
Professional unions	0	1	0	2	0	4	0	3	0
Attitude toward deferment	0	3	0	4	0	2	0	1	0
Subtotal			33		42		39		16

	VALUE SCALE	EMPLOYER A		EMPLOYER B		EMPLOYER C		EMPLOYER D	
THE FIELD									
Growth history	2	2	4	3	6	4	8	1	2
Reaction to business cycles	1	1	1	3	3	4	4	2	2
Future need for goods, services	3	1	3	2	6	4	12	3	9
Subtotal			8		15		24		13
ADVANCEMENT									
Planned training—all levels	3	2	6	3	9	4	12	1	3
Organization for	3	3	9	2	6	4	12	1	3
Regular merit reviews	2	3	6	4	8	1	2	2	4
Advancement from within	2	1	2	3	6	4	8	2	4
Professional employees in top management	1	–	–	–	–	–	–	–	–
Subtotal			23		29		34		14
BENEFITS									
Hospitalization	1	1	1	4	4	3	3	2	2
Life insurance	1	4	4	2	2	1	1	3	3
Retirement	1	2	2	3	3	4	4	1	1
Educational assistance	2	1	2	4	8	3	6	2	4
Vacations	1	4	4	2	2	1	1	3	3
Personal leaves	1	–	–	–	–	–	–	–	–
Sickness and accidents	1	1	1	4	4	3	3	2	2
Military service policies	0	3	0	1	0	4	0	2	0
Recreational plans	0	4	0	1	0	2	0	3	0
Subtotal			14		23		18		15
EXPENSES PAID									
Payment of travel expenses	1	2	2	4	4	3	3	1	1
Payment of moving expenses	2	3	6	4	8	2	4	1	2
Other	–								
Subtotal			8		12		7		3

ADVICE OF OTHERS

	VALUE SCALE	EMPLOYER A		EMPLOYER B		EMPLOYER C		EMPLOYER D	
Faculty	2	3	6	2	4	4	8	1	2
Placement officer	2	3	4	3	6	4	8	1	2
Family	0	2	0	4	0	3	0	1	0
Friends	1	—	—	—	—	—	—	—	—
Subtotal			10		10		16		4

COMPENSATION

	VALUE SCALE	EMPLOYER A		EMPLOYER B		EMPLOYER C		EMPLOYER D	
Salary offered	1	4	4	1	1	2	2	3	3
Savings and stock plan	1	2	2	4	4	3	3	1	1
Bonus history	1	3	3	2	2	4	4	1	1
Product discounts	0	—	—	—	—	—	—	—	—
Cost of living of area	0	3	0	1	0	2	0	4	0
History of general increases	2	1	2	4	8	3	6	2	4
10 years from now—average man	3	2	6	4	12	3	9	1	3
State taxes	1	4	4	2	2	1	1	3	3
Other	—								
Subtotal			21		29		25		15

THE JOB

	VALUE SCALE	EMPLOYER A		EMPLOYER B		EMPLOYER C		EMPLOYER D	
Scope of job	3	4	12	2	6	1	3	3	9
Degree of responsibility	2	4	8	3	6	1	2	2	4
Interest and satisfaction	3	3	9	2	6	4	12	1	3
Travel involved	0	3	0	2	0	1	0	4	0
Prestige of job	1	2	2	4	4	3	3	1	1
Possibility of horizontal moves	1	2	2	3	3	4	4	1	1
Subtotal			23		25		24		18

	VALUE SCALE	EMPLOYER A		EMPLOYER B		EMPLOYER C		EMPLOYER D	
GEOGRAPHICAL LOCATION									
Housing cost	1	3	3	1	1	2	2	4	4
Housing availability	2	2	4	1	2	3	6	4	8
Schools for children	2	3	6	4	8	2	4	1	2
Advanced schools for me	3	1	3	4	12	3	4	2	6
Recreation facilities available	1	1	1	3	3	2	2	4	4
Cultural and religious opportunities	1	2	2	3	3	4	4	1	1
Shopping facilities	0	1	0	4	0	3	0	2	0
Climate	2	2	4	3	6	4	8	1	2
General environment of city and surroundings, etc.	2	3	6	4	8	2	4	1	2
Travel time to work	1	3	3	2	2	1	1	4	4
Transportation facilities from place: highway, rail, air	1	1	1	3	3	4	4	2	2
Other	—								
Subtotal			33		47		44		35
EMPLOYER GRAND TOTALS			213		305		311		180

numerically how much more desirable one employer may be than another. In the comparator shown here, Employer *C* had the highest score (311). However, this was only slightly higher than the score for Employer *B* (305). Employer *A* (213) and Employer *D* (180) were not at all comparable.

Two cautions are important in using rating scales. First, avoid the "halo" effect of letting a generally favorable or unfavorable reaction affect individual ratings. Each individual item should be rated as accurately as possible, regardless of your over-all impression of the organization being rated. Second, rate only factors which you have been able to observe. In the example given, "ratio of professional employees to total," "personal leaves," and "advice of friends" were not rated because of lack of information.

A comparator for rating educational positions has been designed by Brinton Stone of the Office of Educational Placement of the University of California. This particular scale rates college and university positions, although it can be easily adapted to elementary and high school openings. This comparator uses absolute rather than relative ratings. The suggested ratings are Excellent, Good, Fair, Poor, and Bad. Comments or notes may be added to the boxes listing individual ratings (Exhibit 42).

Your best comparator will be one which you develop to fit your field, its job requirements, and your long-range goals. No other yardstick will be as accurate.

WINDING UP YOUR JOB CAMPAIGN

When you have made your decision, the following steps are appropriate:

1. Tell the employer, in writing, that you accept his offer. Remind the employer when and where you will report (e.g., "I shall report to your office at 8 a.m. on Monday, June 26.").

2. Repeat anything you will do prior to reporting for work (i.e., complete a comprehensive biographical form or take a pre-employment physical examination).

3. Restate the salary at which you expect to start. If the position is in an industry which often works more than a forty-hour week (the aircraft and missile field, for example), you may wish to indicate your understanding of the work week upon which your salary is based.

4. Express interest in the opportunity and appreciation for the time, consideration, and assistance given you by the personnel representative. Thanking the personnel man for his time is a basic courtesy.

Once you have accepted a position, stop your job campaign. You are not alone in making an unequivocal decision; your future employer notifies other candidates that the position has been filled. Concentrate your energies on learning more about your new position and preparing for it.

Many graduates anticipate signing a formal contract when they accept a position. Over 80 per cent of all positions in our country are handled without a formal contract. Most organizations accept your verbal or written acceptance as final—and you should assume that your word is as binding as a legally signed document.

To reject a position which you have been offered, or to withdraw your application where it is current, several steps should be taken.

1. Notify the employer, in writing, that you have accepted another position. Repeat the details of the offer or the status of your candidacy to help in your identification.

2. Express appreciation for the consideration you received and, if it is sincere, indicate your respect for the employer's organization.

Exhibit 42 COMPARATOR FOR EDUCATIONAL POSITIONS

	INSTITUTION A	INSTITUTION B	INSTITUTION C	INSTITUTION D
A. GENERAL DESCRIPTION OF THE INSTITUTION				
Identify type (state university, private college, technical institute, etc.)	state college	private college	Private university	state university
Prestige of institution (overall reputation of institution)	2	3	5	3
Eminence of department	1	1	(tops in country?) 5	4
Faculty-administration relationship	4	4	3	2
Faculty-student relationship	2	4	2	1
Type of student body (resident, commuting, evening adult, urban, rural, etc.)	1	5	4	5
Overemphasis upon athletics	4	(no varsity athletics) 5	5	2
SUBTOTAL	14	22	24	17
B. INSTITUTION'S REQUIREMENTS FOR FACULTY MEMBERS				
Doctor's degree required for faculty tenure	4	3	5	5
Emphasis upon research	4	5	2	4
Age requirements	3	4	3	3
Teaching contact hours	3	1	5	4
Experience required	2	3	4	5
Publications required	4	4	2	3
Religious compatibility (if a denominational institution)	—	—	—	—
SUBTOTAL	20	20	21	24
C. MY REQUIREMENTS OF THE INSTITUTION				
Quality, personality, and integrity of the individuals with whom I would be working	3	2	4	3
Quality of laboratory resources in my field	2	1	5	5
Quality of library	1	2	5	4

	INSTITUTION A	INSTITUTION B	INSTITUTION C	INSTITUTION D
Method of financing department (outside sources of support?)	2	1	5	4
Flexibility of department budget	1	1	3	4
Type of work being done by closest probable colleagues	2	1	5	5
SUBTOTAL	11	8	27	25
D. FRINGE BENEFITS				
Sabbatical leaves	4	2	5	5
Tenure rules	2	4	4	5
Travel funds	1	1	5	4
Retirement program	4	2	4	3
Insurance programs	2	3	3	4
Summer session jobs	4	1	5	3
Sick-leave policy	3	4	3	4
Housing aid	2	5	1	3
Leaves to attend professional meetings	1	2	5	5
SUBTOTAL	23	24	35	36
E. PERSONAL REQUIREMENTS				
Salary	4	1	4	5
Cost of living in area	1	4	2	4
Cost of moving	3	1	5	1
Housing available	2	5	1	3
Tax rates	3	2	4	5
Character of community (industrial, rural, etc.)	4	4	3	2
Quality of schools	4	2	3	3
Walk or drive to work, or public transportation	3	5	1	4
Distance from home town	1	1	4	3
Distance from metropolitan area and services	4	2	5	2
Climate (heat, cold, rain, humidity)	5	5	2	3
Recreational opportunities	4	5	3	1
Public services	2	1	5	5
Degree of autonomy in work	4	5	3	2
Satisfactory office conditions	3	4	5	2
Reaction to whole situation after personal visit to campus	1	5	5	2
SUBTOTAL	48	52	55	47

	INSTITUTION A	INSTITUTION B	INSTITUTION C	INSTITUTION D
F. ULTIMATE GOALS				
Possibility of promotion. Can I move from here with ease to another institution?	3	2	5	4
Would I be content to stay here if I advance at a reasonable rate and like the job?	2	2	5	4
SUBTOTAL	5	4	10	8
TOTAL POINTS	121	130	172	157

3. State briefly the position you accepted. Employers are naturally curious to learn what you accepted.
4. Phrase your letter carefully to close the door gently. If you apply at a later date, your present letter of rejection should help your future cause.
5. Notify your college placement office, private employment agency, or other employment sources of your decision. This will be appreciated by them, permit completion of your records, and allow these agencies to devote their energies to candidates who need assistance.
6. Thoughtful candidates thank their references for their help and inform them of the position accepted.

Many candidates start working too soon, as if motivated by the fear that their position will evaporate unless they report for work immediately. Other men and women are anxious to get on a payroll as soon as possible, although they might be happier and start work better prepared after a short vacation. They allow no time for possible delays caused by moving vans or for difficulties in locating suitable housing.

If you are changing positions, give your current employer at least two weeks' notice of your intention to leave. Any shorter notice makes it difficult to secure your replacement, leaves your current responsibilities uncovered, and handicaps future recommendations from this employer. Occasionally an employer may agree to a shorter period—but this should be his decision, not yours. Your future employer will have greater respect for your sense of loyalty if you insist on giving and serving your two weeks' notice. Persons serving under a formally signed contract should be prepared to complete their prescribed tour of service.

Obtaining the right position is only a stage in proper career planning. Successfully launching your career and making the most of your opportunities for advancement are the subjects covered in the balance of this book.

PART THREE:
EVALUATING
YOUR PROGRESS

CHAPTER 14

THE TRAINING PERIOD

The change from a college campus to an employing organization may be an abrupt one. You are no longer in the top rank reserved for college seniors. Like a freshman, you must start over again in a situation in which you must prove yourself. The process is similar to that used by sororities and fraternities. First the red carpet is rolled out to entice you to join. Then you go through the trials and tribulations of pledgeship (the training period) until finally you merit complete acceptance as a member of the organization.

Many graduates fail to plan beyond the job campaign.

YOUR INITIAL ORIENTATION

Your first day may be your hardest. As a new employee, you may not have enough to do and may spend much of your time waiting for instructions. The people around you will be busy with their regular work and may not have adequate time to talk with you.

Your attitude should be friendly and courteous but not familiar. Learn the names, job functions, and personalities of those with whom you may be working.

Don't be disappointed if you are not making direct use of your college training or professional abilities in your first months on the job. College graduates often chafe at the early restrictions. "How can I get experience" the graduate asks, "if you don't try me on the job?"

W. L. McGrath, president of the Williamson Heater Company and past presi-

dent of the National Society for Advancement of Management, makes this point:

What would you think if the Air Force gave a man an intensive classroom instruction in flying—and then without his ever having been in a plane before, put him in the pilot's seat and expected him to take off over a mountain range? You would say it was suicide. And that's what happens to a man who is given a position of responsibility before he is ready for it.

It's when a man is ready and is finally given a chance at responsibility that what he has learned in school proves out. For then he is able to interpret theory in the light of practical working knowledge. . . . It's a matter of statistics that in management, college-trained men may not get off to a much faster start than the others—*but they go further in the long run.*

Learn internal practices. Even the simple coffee break operates under both a written and unwritten law. Are breaks permitted? When? How long do they last? May you leave the building? With whom do you rotate work coverage?

Rigid customs often pertain to minor matters. One male graduate made the mistake of sitting at the same luncheon table with some of the young ladies from his office only to learn he had violated an unwritten law of the office. It took months to live down his Don Juan reputation.

Sam N. Wolk, former director of college relations and recruitment for the U.S. Civil Service Commission, sums up his advice to trainees in these words:

Expect to encounter delays occasioned by channels of communication or chains of command. Organizational structure may seem cumbersome, but it serves a useful purpose. It prevents those at the top from being bogged down with details and frees them for the planning and directing job they're paid to do.

Expect to attend seemingly interminable conferences and committee meetings. Boring many of them may be and some may result in only a decision to hold another meeting. However, no other device has yet been invented which is a more efficient medium for communicating ideas and arriving at operationally sound decisions.

Don't expect to be formulating policy six months after you start work—you will be most unusual and successful if you're doing it six years from now. You'd really better plan on sixteen.

Don't lose sight of "the big picture." But, on the other hand, don't be so enamored of it that you neglect to master the details of your part of the canvas. To be blunt—learn your job and learn it well. You will never be of value to any organization otherwise.

Expect to be assigned occasionally to tasks below your dignity and capabilities. When it happens, don't become convinced that your talents are not appreciated. It's just that those jobs have to be done from time to time and they historically have been assigned to "the new man."

Expect to have your suggestions for improvement turned down firmly and not always politely. Don't form the opinion that your superiors are bumbling idiots of no vision who reached their positions of eminence either through sordid conniving or through the grace of an otherwise intelligent God. They just possibly may know more and have better judgment than you think. They may also have learned through bitter experience that the sweeping changes you advocate might bring the organization to the brink of embarrassment, if not of disaster.

Develop a sensitivity to your supervisor and the organization. It is far easier to make adjustments than it is to reshape people's attitudes or organizational inertia.

FORMAL TRAINING

Employees are usually the key to an organization's success. Andrew Carnegie, the steel king, made the classic comment: "Take away our money, our great works, our mines, and coke ovens, but leave our organization and in four years I shall have reestablished myself."

Many organizations consider training one of their most valuable investments in the future. Typical is the Insurance Company of North America which has thirteen teachers in its education department.

Your formal training may not begin the day you start work. Some organizations wait until a group of new employees is available before starting training sessions. Pending the start of the training program, new employees are assigned basic positions through which they obtain on-the-job experience.

Training programs are designed:

1. To integrate most efficiently the large numbers of new graduates hired each year.
2. To provide new graduates with background information on the organization similar to that gained in the past by men who worked their way up.
3. To make high-salaried new college graduates productive as soon as possible.

The three common methods of training college graduates are rotational work assignments, formal classroom courses, and on-the-job training. These methods are used individually or in combination.

Rotational work assignments provide a first-hand picture of each department and its personnel. Most employers feel that work in a department provides better training than does mere observation.

Formal classroom courses permit group orientation. Classes include lectures, seminars, discussions, reading assignments, and films on the employing organization, its products or services, and its administrative structure. They are often scheduled during the initial weeks of employment or during evening meetings.

On-the-job training is the oldest and simplest method of orientation. The new employee learns by doing, using a formal training manual or working under supervision.

Typical training programs of employers in various fields are described in Exhibit 43.

HOW TO SUCCEED AS A TRAINEE

Attitude is important. A leading training director said: "After watching thousands of trainees in business succeed or fail, I have become convinced that attitude is the key, the denominator of success. However, I know how easy it is for us trainers to lose sight of attitude while busily engaged in imparting knowledge and skill."*

Pay particular attention to your fellow employees. Careers have been made or broken by the ability to work effectively with other people. Too many college graduates move in a tight circle with each other. You will be a broader and richer person working and mixing with all levels of employees, and your future success will depend upon how well you motivate all employees to want to work with you.

You must develop your own ideas and learn how and when to present them. Employers differ in their encouragement of critical thinking on the part of trainees. Some employers request written reports describing and evaluating each department through which a trainee passes. Other organizations assume the graduate is limited to a learning situation.

Be sensitive to the proper balance between alert critical thinking and the need

* H. Paul Abbott, "The Common Denominator of Success," *Journal of College Placement,* March, 1956, p. 9.

Exhibit 43 TYPICAL TRAINING PROGRAMS

PROCTER & GAMBLE COMPANY

"On-the-job training with direct job assignment and early assumption of responsibility characterizes the training philosophy of Procter & Gamble. Learning by doing distinguishes all the individualized P&G training programs in such areas as manufacturing, research and development, engineering, advertising, sales, purchasing, and finance.

"Typical is the production training program in manufacturing which is designed to prepare the new man to assume full responsibility for an operating department in approximately four months. The newly hired graduate is told immediately of his initial management assignment and his training is directed toward preparation for it.

"Training in production is built around approximately 125 short, project-type assignments selected by the man's immediate supervisor. Each assignment provides either basic job information, practice in management skills, or both. While each trainee is encouraged to assume some responsibility for his own training, the basic responsibility for training the new man rests with his immediate supervisor."

WESTINGHOUSE ELECTRIC CORPORATION

"Westinghouse hires nearly all of its inexperienced young professional personnel for its Graduate Training Program rather than for a specific job. Eventual placement within the Westinghouse organization follows completion of initial training and a fuller assessment of the graduate's abilities: While it is not possible at the beginning of training to predict which job an individual will take, it is certain that at least one opening exists for each man recruited.

"Each graduate begins his training at the Westinghouse Educational Center located in suburban Pittsburgh. Three weeks of 'Operation Westinghouse' provides a clear picture of the organization of the Corporation, its future objectives, and the career channels open to him. He has the opportunity to meet with and discuss technical problems and company philosophy with a number of top management officials.

"Each graduate plans a program with his training supervisor which will consist of rotational work assignments and integrated classroom work. The assignments provide both valuable experience and bring him in contact with senior professional people. The classroom work provides additional information on operating procedure and policies, solving case problems, and applying educational background to practice.

"While the length of the training program varies with the graduate's prior experience and maturity, it usually lasts six months. Upon completion of training, the graduate becomes a permanent member of one of the departments in which he received training. Usually, the trainee has a choice of several permanent positions."

LOS ANGELES COUNTY

"One of the best organized municipal government training programs is conducted by Los Angeles County, which started its first program in 1933. Distinctly different courses are arranged for Personnel Trainees, Probation Trainees, Trainee Appraisers, and Administrative Trainees.

"The one-year Administrative Trainee course acquaints young graduates with the organizational structure and operations of the municipal government, through lectures and informal discussions with County executives, field trips, and office visits.

"Each trainee receives personalized work assignments which may involve budget preparation and analysis, systems and procedures analysis, operation and manpower studies, and workflow and organizational studies. Periodic seminars are held to permit trainees to discuss their individual assignments and develop conference techniques."

MERRILL LYNCH, PIERCE, FENNER, & SMITH

"Merrill Lynch uses two programs to equip men for positions in its organization. These are the Junior Executive Program (for college graduates entering the brokerage business) and the Sales Training Program (for college graduates with two or more years business experience and a defined interest in the investment business). Graduates interested in Securities Research enter directly into a one-year on-the-job training course.

"The Junior Executive Training Program is a 21-month combination of on-the-job and academic training for men who usually have had little knowledge of the securities business. Trainees observe and perform work in various departments of the firm. Three months of intensive classroom work cover underwriting, security analysis, public speaking, accounting, sales techniques, and corporation finance."

BERKELEY PUBLIC SCHOOL SYSTEM

"New teachers meet for a week prior to the beginning of the school year. During this week they learn the System's educational philosophy, operating principles, and administrative techniques. This orientation includes meeting with the superintendent of schools, supervisors of specialized subject-matter fields, and school principals. Visits to schools are arranged.

On the last day each new instructor moves into his new classroom to organize it for his teaching assignments.

"During the first year, the new teacher works closely with the principal, specialized supervisory personnel, and consulting teachers."

U.S. SOCIAL SECURITY ADMINISTRATION

"Men and women selected for training with the Bureau of Old-Age and Survivors Insurance of the Social Security Administration may enter directly through the Federal Service Entrance Examination or qualify for more extensive training by passing also the Management Intern Option of this examination.

"Most new Bureau employees selected through the FSEE general examination start in one of three training assignments: claims representative, claims authorizer, or adjustment examiner.

"Persons who are selected as a result of the Management Intern examination enter a 24-month training program conducted in Baltimore. The first three months are devoted to an orientation program which includes: (1) a three-week course covering the history, philosophy, organizational structure, and legislation under which the Bureau operates, (2) a short technical training course in the mechanics and procedures of the social security claims process, (3) field visits to a district office and a payment center, (4) and a final course dealing with principles of management, organizational analysis, and budget administration and their practical application to problems faced by the Bureau."

ABRAHAM & STRAUS

"About 60 young men and women are admitted each year to the department store's Executive Training Squad. Formal training consists of classroom work and supervised experience on the selling floor, with section managers, in buyers' offices, and in behind-the-scenes departments. Weekly assignments during the first four to eight weeks are devoted to the subject of selling; then come four weeks of section manager training and experience, followed by a six weeks' period on merchandise training (assistant buyer training). After six months in the Squad, trainees are transferred to Graduate Training status and are placed in a specific junior executive position as openings occur in the field in which they are most interested."

STANDARD OIL COMPANY OF CALIFORNIA

"Training is primarily on the job and is conducted by the division in which the new employee works. Job rotation is provided within the division and, in several programs, temporary developmental assignments are made on an exchange basis with other parts of the company.

"Graduates hired by the Engineering Department begin productive work almost immediately. First, however, the graduate studies the organization of his department and his division, meets the men in his department and division management, and discusses his initial project assignments.

"During the first year, the graduate visits some oil fields and tours the Richmond refinery. Three weeks are spent in a drafting orientation program. During the first year, trainees attend periodic seminars describing department activity and relationships."

---

to develop sufficient background knowledge of an organization before you become one of its critics. Without appearing critical, you may be able to present your ideas tactfully through the questions you ask. You should never need to comment negatively on the work of your predecessor.

Don't expect your employer to cram all necessary knowledge into you. You must assume a major portion of the responsibility for your own training. In addition to the formal training you receive at your employer's instigation, look around for supplementary sources of the information you will find essential and useful in your career.

Ask yourself this question: Will the complete training program prepare for top performance in meeting the demands anticipated in the future? If not, where may additional training be received?

Conflicting demands on your time will inevitably develop between the interests of your family and the professional demands of your career. This problem is heightened for many graduates who begin both their career and their married life at the same time. In this respect, past generations were fortunate: Economic necessity forced a postponement of marriage until permitted by career stability and income level.

Both husband and wife must recognize the importance of a sound career beginning, even if it involves sacrificing some of the time they might spend together. You

may have to work or study overtime as you learn new assignments or devote some evenings to night courses.

Salary is worth a long-range view. Most employees are not eligible for a salary adjustment until they have worked six to twelve months. Larger employers often follow a systematic plan of salary increments during the first several years. After this period, earnings begin to reflect individual merit.

One young trainee dashed into his supervisor's office armed with statistics showing how he could not live on his present salary. This was a disastrous experiment. His supervisor had to follow the firm's salary schedule, and this incident marred their relationship for months.

The first year on a new job may prove to be a "honeymoon." Your production goals are usually low, your assignments often are noncontroversial, and your superiors and colleagues are generally willing to give you the benefit of the doubt if mistakes appear in your work.

Too many young graduates assume that their careers will always be smooth and their positions undemanding. Unfortunately, work assignments increase in difficulty and your employer will expect more from your performance. You may agree with the graduate who said, "attempting to keep up with the demands of my position is like trying to take a drink out of a firehose."

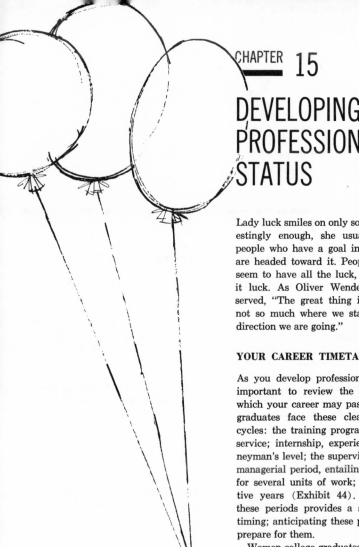

CHAPTER 15

DEVELOPING PROFESSIONAL STATUS

Lady luck smiles on only some of us. Interestingly enough, she usually smiles on people who have a goal in life—and who are headed toward it. People with a goal seem to have all the luck, if you can call it luck. As Oliver Wendell Holmes observed, "The great thing in the world is not so much where we stand as in what direction we are going."

YOUR CAREER TIMETABLE

As you develop professional status, it is important to review the stages through which your career may pass. Most college graduates face these clearly observable cycles: the training program and military service; internship, experience on a journeyman's level; the supervisory phase; the managerial period, entailing responsibility for several units of work; and the executive years (Exhibit 44). Understanding these periods provides a sense of career timing; anticipating these periods helps to prepare for them.

Women college graduates generally have a different timetable for their careers. The majority will work for two or three years and then start another career as homemaker; they may or may not reenter the labor force when the children have grown up. Traditions and prejudices against women in responsible positions will slow up their timetable in many organizations. Most important from the career planning concept is the fact that women do not have the same viewpoint nor the same motivations as men toward concern over long-range career plans. However, for those who plan a career, the same principles prove helpful as for men.

The *training* period includes not only the experiences suggested in Chapter 14, but also the trial-and-error experiences obtained from personal participation. The amount of formal training the new teacher receives on the job will vary, but the beginning teacher will definitely learn from experience how to prepare more efficiently for classes, how to maintain discipline among students, and how to get along with older teachers and administrators. In government and business it is common to expose graduates to some type of training to hasten the time when they will earn their salaries. Men facing a military obligation find military service better timed when it occurs during the training period than later, when it may have a more damaging effect on advancement possibilities.

The period of *internship* is the "journeyman" level when you are expected to begin to perform competently in your field. The salesman, for example, is expected to work on his own initiative and know how to develop prospects, plan calls efficiently, maintain accurate records, persuade the customer, and close the order. During this period you are expected to develop your proficiency in your own field and begin to demonstrate your ability to get results.

During the latter part of your internship period, you will be watched for any evidence of *supervisory* ability. First promotions to important supervisory positions occur around the age of thirty. This will be the first test of your ability to get results through others; the manner in which you accept responsibility and accomplish work assignments will have a lasting effect upon your long-range career plans. Basic work skills and background knowledge acquired in the internship years will be nurtured during this period of your career. Your knowledge of psychology and principles of management and your own innate ability and common sense should be utilized to show your superiors that you have the talent for planning, motivating people, and getting results.

During the *managerial or minor executive* years, you should be on the threshold of major opportunities. Your work should increasingly involve responsibility for several operating units. If you have been progressing toward your career goal effectively and on schedule, you will have developed a reputation in your own organization and in your business or industry for getting things done. You should find opportunities commensurate with your abilities either through internal promotion or alternative employment opportunities.

If by age forty your achievements do not justify consideration for promotion to major *executive* status, your chances of reaching this goal become increasingly poorer. Your pattern of success and pro-

Exhibit 44 STAGES IN THE COLLEGE GRADUATE'S CAREER

AGE	CAREER STAGE
22–24	Training program (and military service)
25–30	Internship (experience on a journeyman's level)
31–35	Supervisory (getting work done through others)
36–40	Managerial or minor executive (responsibility for several units of work)
41 on	Executive (peak years of performance)

motions up to this age should suggest whether you have leveled off and reached the peak of your performance or whether additional promotions still lie ahead.

As your career develops, you should concentrate on (1) developing yourself, (2) making your own breaks, (3) crystallizing a personal philosophy, and (4) taking inventory.

DEVELOPING YOURSELF

Abraham Lincoln said, "You do not help a man when you do for him what he can and should do for himself." Most employers agree. They speak of their responsibility for executive development but, when pressed, will admit that the men they want to promote will really develop themselves.

There are many methods through which you may develop yourself.

You should broaden your perspective. To merit promotions, you need the ability to look at problems from a management, rather than an employee, viewpoint. The broad perspective shows why things are done in a certain way. An old adage states:

The person who knows *how* will always have a job,

But the person who knows *why* will generally be his boss.

The higher you go, the more important is the ability to assume a project, execute it, and complete it.

Complete minor as well as major assignments. One personnel officer was highly impressed by the task performed by his college-trained secretary. She was asked to see if a group of overseas visitors might attend an evening meeting in Minneapolis and arrive at an industrial plant in the Chicago suburbs by noon the next day. Rather than presenting brief data from available airplane and railroad timetables, this young lady inquired about available space and summarized the alternatives.

She also recommended the selected course of action—that the visitors take a night Pullman train which would provide the maximum amount of time in Minneapolis, allow eight hours for sleep, and discharge the visitors in the Chicago suburbs near the plant at 8:30 A.M. instead of requiring a long trip out from the Loop.

Consider your social impression. Success in interpersonal relationships with your boss, fellow employees, and customers is of primary importance. Are you able to adjust to the pressures of your job while retaining your cheerfullness and humility.

Ben Franklin said that "success has ruined many a man." Success may result in promotions over many of your friends and colleagues. You should treat them with respect and recognize that they may look upon your success with some envy. Without being sanctimonious, an attitude of humility toward your achievement is usually more effective than one of too obvious relish for your new power or responsibility.

Develop a satisfactory life outside. Success on the job is most likely to come to a person who also succeeds off the job. Personal relationships and personal finances should not interfere with job performance—and will not, if handled successfully. A wife is not a management consultant. Unpaid personal bills are not a company problem.

Use academic courses to aid your self-development. Too many college graduates assume that commencement is the end of formal study rather than a stage in the educational process. The holder of a bachelor's degree should not be complacent about his academic preparation. The number of college graduates may double between 1960 and 1970. Possession of a master's or doctor's degree becomes increasingly helpful. For every 100 bachelor's degrees awarded today, 19 persons receive master's degrees and 2 receive the doctorate.

Additional education is a further investment in your future, providing it is directed wisely. But as Boynton says, "Aimless study, like aimless job hunting, is a waste of energy and time, not to say money. If you are going to study, *study with a purpose* . . . relate your study to your work and to the changing course of the world in which you live."*

Employers often assist financially. For example, if the course should contribute to an improvement in work activities, the Weyerhaeuser Timber Company pays the first $25 of course cost, plus 50 per cent of the remainder upon completion of the course. The Chase Manhattan Bank refunds 100 per cent of the tuition fee upon successful completion of courses which are directly related to the individual's position and career in banking.

Over eighty educational institutions offer training courses for young executives which carry the label "advanced management." Typical is the Columbia University–operated series "Executive Program in Business Administration," held at Arden House, Harriman, New York. This six-week course includes lectures, case studies, discussions, and full use of library resources. The participants average twenty to twenty-five years of experience.

Larger organizations often offer their own courses, taught by employees or by faculty members from nearby universities. Goodyear Tire and Rubber Company offers courses on a wide variety of subjects, both technical and nontechnical. Many of these courses are directed to the individual and his self-development rather than to his current position. Some of the courses are Creative Thinking, Let's Write Better Letters, and Personal Economics.

The capstone of training in the General Electric Company is provided by the Advanced Management Institute established in 1956. Located in a specially built facil-

* Paul W. Boynton, *So You Want a Better Job*, Socony Mobil Oil Company, Inc., New York, p. 10. (Out of print.)

ity at rural Crotonville, New York, this nine-week course is developed to produce the large number of managers needed to run General Electric's highly decentralized organization. According to course manager James M. Shipton, the course is designed to (1) provide time for thought free from the distractions of family responsibility, everyday work responsibilities, and even the enticements of a metropolitan area; (2) to bring executives into stimulating contact with each other; (3) to permit the opportunity for serious reading, aided by two thoroughly stocked libraries; and (4) to encourage this group in its development through use of a faculty skilled in lecture sessions, augmented by visiting lecturers from universities and other organizations.

Interestingly enough, the course theme is not how to produce improved products or greater profits, but a basically philosophical study of the relationship of the General Electric Company to the world environment in which it operates. Participants study the role of the corporation from political, economic, social, and ethical standpoints to develop a personal philosophy of management responsibility.

Many professional associations have established programs to help employees develop their talent. The American Management Association operates three educational centers (located in New York City, Lake Saranac, New York, and on the campus of Colgate University) which annually offer management training to 70,-000 aspiring executives.

Although training is available today to a greater extent than ever before in history, only one person in ten makes use of training opportunities to increase his value to his employer.

MAKING YOUR OWN BREAKS

A well-known axiom in the sports field is "A good team makes its own breaks." Yet one hears "It's not what you know, it's who you know." Two stories may help to point out the role of breaks in a career. *Fortune* related that in 1956 "General Motors disclosed that LeRoy Curtice, brother of GM's President Harlow Curtice (whose own 1956 income totaled $775,000) was being retired by the corporation with a pension of $63 a month after serving twenty-eight years as a GM paint and metal inspector."*

One of the most sensational cases of intervention on the part of a high official occurred in the military world. Sensing the leadership of a forty-six-year-old regular Army captain, one President of the United States sought a method of recognizing his worth. By law, the President has no way of affecting Army promotions, except at the rank of general. The President gave this officer his big break by promoting him over 862 senior officers from captain to brigadier general. The President was Theodore Roosevelt and the Army officer was John J. Pershing. Was this a "break" or recognition of potential ability?

The following suggestions should help you earn your own breaks.

Select your work assignments. Your daily duties are determined by your supervisor. On a long-range basis, however, you can aid your advancement by requesting transfers to other departments, appointments to certain committees, and volunteering to do jobs requiring contact with other areas. To make effective use of this suggestion, first study the promotional channels in your organization and try to chart them. Career patterns in typical fields are presented in Exhibit 45.

A young assistant professor volunteered to represent his department on a university-wide public relations committee. He soon became chairman of the committee. His interest and skill in this area led to his acceptance of the position of public relations director of the university.

A maxim for those interested in public school administration is to become an administrator—even if it means a half-time principalship in a small rural high school. The skills learned, the actual practice in administration, and the observable record of achievement provide a starting point for an administrative career. School systems often favor persons with administrative experience rather than a straight teaching record.

No one path marks the career patterns of successful executives. The book *The Executive Life*† delved into the work histories of 900 top executives. Their paths were diverse. Sales was the chief function prior to assuming top leadership for 25 per cent of the executives. A background in production and operations was second at 23 per cent. Other main areas were: finance, 16 per cent; general management, 16 per cent; engineering and research, 11 per cent; law, 8 per cent; and other, 1 per cent.

Should you seek staff or line responsibilities? The distinction between staff and line work is clearest in military organization. Persons with staff responsibilities become experts in special areas on which they provide advice. Officers with line responsibilities personally direct operations. In more simple terms, the staff-line concept may be described as a planner-executer team. While many organizations select top management from among those with a strong line background, a combination of both line and staff experience provides excellent background for top-level assignments.

Many graduates lack sufficient patience. Most new positions involve difficulties. Judging a career opportunity in less than a year is like attempting to evaluate your choice of a college in October of your freshman year.

Robert Hilkert, a vice-president of the

* Perrin Stryker, "Would You Hire Your Son?" *Fortune,* March, 1957, p. 223.

† Editors of *Fortune, The Executive Life,* Doubleday & Company, Inc., New York, 1956, p. 31.

Exhibit 45 CAREER PATTERNS IN TYPICAL FIELDS

AGE	Salesman	Federal Government Employee	Engineer	Teacher	Office Worker	Retailer
50	Regional Sales Manager	Bureau Chief	Plant Manager	Principal (large school)	Office Manager	Sectional Merchandise Manager
45	Assistant Regional Sales Manager		Assistant Plant Manager			
					Secretary	
40	District Manager	Assistant Bureau Chief	Chief Engineer	Principal (small school)	Raising Family	Buyer (large department)
35	Assistant District Manager		Assistant Chief Engineer	Assistant Principal		Buyer (small department)
30	Sales Supervisor	Senior Budget Examiner	Department Engineer			Assistant Buyer
25	Salesman	Budget Examiner	Project Engineer	Teacher	Executive Secretary	Section Supervisor
	Trainee		Military Service		Secretary	Sales
	Military Service	Trainee	Trainee	Master's Degree	Stenographer	Trainee
22	Master's Degree	Master's Degree				

Graduation from College

Career Fields: Salesman, Federal Government Employee, Engineer, Teacher, Office Worker, Retailer

Federal Reserve Bank of Philadelphia and a lecturer at Temple University, has this tip to offer:*

It is usually easier for you to modify your needs than it is for the company to change its regulations. Companies are funny that way. Somehow they seem not to possess the flexibility that enables them to tailor-make their requirements to the desires of the new employee. Though you may be filled with management knowledge and busting at the seams with modern ideas, you will serve your interests best by appearing on the scene as a learner rather than as a management consultant.

Many covet a headquarters assignment too early in their career. They assume that possession of a title, such as "assistant to the president," will help them get ahead. Being known by top executives is helpful, but jobs are usually filled by those with proven management experience.

Almost every day you will have opportunities to demonstrate your initiative and enthusiasm. The seal of the Carnegie Institute of Technology bears the motto "My heart is in the work," attributed to Andrew Carnegie. Obviously, you must be enthusiastic for your work to be successful. Exhibit 46 tells a story of initiative on the job.

You should avoid internal politics. Rightly or wrongly, many organizations are divided into cliques. Sometimes this division stems from the staffs of second-line executives competing for promotion. Other groups form around high-status employees or natural leaders.

Graduates should be sensitive to organization politics, but avoid participation themselves. Internal politics often deal with petty problems; there is no need to compromise your own set of values by becoming involved in them.

* Robert N. Hilkert, "Tips to a College Man Going to Work," *Personnel Journal*, May, 1954, p. 11.

On one of its monthly calendars, the KVP-Sutherland Paper Company presents this slogan:

Great Minds Discuss Ideas
Average Minds Discuss Events
Little Minds Discuss People

Understanding your supervisor is important in working effectively with and under him. You must be flexible.

Typical was the graduate whose first two supervisors had conflicting views. One said, "My men are doing their jobs if they are away from their desks. I expect them to be out in the plant, not sitting around waiting for phone calls. My men are expected to do their reading at night, not at their desks." By contrast, his next supervisor said, "I want to keep my people at my fingertips. They should be available at a moment's notice to help with crises as they develop. If I get a call from New York requesting immediate attention to a problem, I want to be able to literally reach over, tap my subordinates on the shoulder and tell them what I need."

Many graduates find it helpful to select a model and attempt to learn from his principles, techniques, and professional success. This model may be your supervisor or a particularly effective employee. No one is perfect, so emulate your model's good points and try to avoid his weaknesses.

You should advertise your abilities. You may remember the story of Ensign Pulver in the play *Mister Roberts*. Ensign Pulver was so afraid of the commander of his Navy cargo ship that he avoided being seen by the captain for fourteen months. Obviously Pulver was not interested in getting ahead, for one has to be seen to be appreciated.

Some years ago a young bank teller became noted for the fine chorus which he directed at the employees' Christmas party. In time, all the senior officers learned his name. Knowing his name, they were able to identify his work, which was excellent. As a result, he received numerous promotions and at the time of his retirement was serving as senior vice-president.

A well-organized written report advertises your abilities. Written materials provide evidence for your supervisor to back up his recommendation concerning your future assignments.

Effective public speaking also helps to advertise your abilities. Formal talks to outside groups will enhance your reputation, but your contribution to committees within your organization may be of even greater importance. Your supervisor has to initiate the action for your promotion, so your contribution to committees to which he assigns you may be more important than outside activities.

Keep careful records. You should maintain a continuous portfolio. Letters of commendation, newspaper clippings, or reports which show your ability should be carefully filed for the day when you may wish evidence of your performance. You may spend your entire career with your current employer. Should you wish to change—or if you are interviewed for a transfer or promotional opportunity within your present organization—documentation of your success will prove a helpful asset.

CRYSTALLIZING A PERSONAL PHILOSOPHY

As you mature, you become unique. By the time of its twenty-fifth reunion, members of a college class who were once quite similar will have developed in different

Exhibit 46 INITIATIVE IN ACTION

Three brothers went to work for the same company at the same salary. A year later, one was getting $400 a month, the second $500, and the third $700. Their father felt this was unfair and went to his sons' boss to find out why. "I'll let them explain why," said the boss. He then called each son in turn, and told him this story: "I understand the Oceanic has just docked. I want you to go down to the pier and get an inventory of her cargo."

Jim, the lowest paid man, got the story in three minutes. "She carries 2000 seal skins," he said. "I got that from the first mate over the phone."

Frank, the $500 man, took an hour. He came back with a list showing 2000 seal skins, 500 beaver and 11 mink pelts.

George, the $700 man, didn't return for three hours. "The Oceanic carries 2000 seal skins," he began. "They can be had at $5 each, so I took a two-day option and wired a prospect in St. Louis. I think he'll buy at $7 if that's OK with you. I found 500 beaver pelts aboard: I've learned through a phone call we can sell at a $700 profit if you agree. There are also 11 mink pelts aboard, but they're of poor quality, so I didn't try to do anything with them."

Source: "Embree Chips," New Britain Machine Company, New Britain, Conn.

ways. This diversity stems from specialized vocational and personal experience and from different personal philosophies.

A well-developed personal philosophy crystallizes attitudes toward problems and help the individual to reach decisions. How one operates professionally and how one lives personally combine to determine this philosophy, and it is reflected in your attitudes toward other people and their attitude toward you.

Hilkert has this to say on the qualities of leadership: *

One of the first signs of . . . emerging leadership [is] the ability to win the respect of any group in which [you happen] to be placed. This respect comes when others realize that you respect them for their knowledge and experience, when they feel that you appreciate their efforts in your behalf, when they come to realize that you are a *real person,* and that you are more interested in them and in the general welfare than you are in yourself. Your job as a future manager is not to bid openly for the attention of the big boss. Rather it is to win a place in the hearts of the rank and file.

Do you treat your subordinates the way you expect to be treated yourself? Do you spend as much time with them as with your superior? Do you care as much about their future success as you hope your superior cares about yours?

The most valuable employees think constantly of problems from their employer's viewpoint. Would you operate a division at average efficiency, or would you—through more personal effort—strive to improve its efficiency? Do you cooperate fully with other divisions to improve the job of the total organization? Do you al-

ways consider the long-range implications of your actions?

Everett Reese, former president of the American Bankers Association, said, "College graduates had the rights and privileges of this country; they also have the responsibility to continue these rights and privileges for the benefit of their successors." Graduating students are often willing to dedicate themselves to improving society; ten years after graduation, these attitudes will have disappeared unless the service concept is ingrained in their personal philosophy of life.

You did not make the world, you inherited it. Yet you cannot escape your obligation to help maintain its moral standards.

In a speech to undergraduates at Williams College, Robert L. Fegley spoke of ethics in business:

When you enter the business world, you will find many effective restraints that work to keep businessmen honest and responsible.

The most important is your personal standard of morality. You will be working among persons, who, like yourself, have grown up in the Judaeo-Christian ethical tradition that is characteristic of our country, and who have the same general standards of right and wrong. To maintain your self-respect, you will probably try to make morally sound decisions.

But there is an additional dimension —your responsibility to your associates. You are the representative of a business firm, and what you do in this capacity reflects to the credit or discredit of the company. Competitive pressures or personal ambitions might tempt a man to cut corners ethically, but he would find an extra deterrent in the thought that his action could injure the reputation of the company and hurt everyone connected with it.

* Robert N. Hilkert, "Tips to a College Man Going to Work," *Personnel Journal,* May, 1954, p. 11.

TAKING INVENTORY

Your work performance will constantly be appraised by your supervisors—whether formally or informally. This appraisal may result in the extension of a teaching contract for the next school year. It may be a periodic performance review in a governmental agency, or a business firm's evaluation of several candidates for a single promotional opportunity. Unfortunately, in some cases the only way to tell whether or not your work has been satisfactory is to wait until you receive a salary increase. Regardless of external evaluations, you should seek your own appraisals.

You may profitably review your performance on three bases: (1) comparison of results with employer statements made during the hiring process, (2) discussion of progress with supervisor, and (3) self-analysis.

An applicant who took careful notes (either mentally or in writing) during the selection process would know what was expected of him at various stages of his career, what kinds of training and assignments he could receive, and what form of review or salary consideration he should anticipate.

A frank discussion of your performance with your immediate supervisor should help in your appraisal. Supervisors are normally reluctant to talk about your weak points, but will probably do so at your request.

Many young graduates assume that their work is satisfactory merely because of the absence of any negative reports. They are often shocked to learn that the supervisor simply had not taken time to share criticisms with them. Acceptance of this advice, and an attitude of appreciation for it, may prompt other suggestions designed to improve your training, experience, and performance.

Employers often make a deliberate attempt to evaluate a man's performance early in his career. Their goal is to weed out the least qualified as soon as possible, permitting them to relocate before losing time.

While your supervisor may rate your work as satisfactory, your future plans usually depend upon receiving a better-than-average evaluation. The "gentleman's C" may have qualified for graduation from college, but it will not lead to many promotions.

The most complete appraisal is the one you make yourself. This is done by determining the answer to questions such as these:

1. Does your work challenge all of your abilities? Do you really enjoy going to work in the morning? Do you feel able to handle the even more difficult assignments to which advancement would lead?

2. Are you able to make the decisions necessary in your field? Do you obtain and use accurate background information to help in making decisions?

3. Are you able to accept the criticism which accompanies advancement? Do you have enough inner drive, strength of conviction, and enthusiasm for your work to move forward confidently despite external criticism? A radio station executive recently sought a position in another field. As he was technically competent, each job began smoothly. When normal criticism began to develop, however, he found his ideas inhibited, his enthusiasm dimmed, and his creativity numbed by excessive caution.

4. Are you able to sort out important ideas and present them tactfully and effectively? Do you practice economy in words, both written and spoken? Loquaciousness is a common handicap of the unsuccessful.

5. Are you succeeding without undue dependence upon argument? You must ration your use of argument or run the

risk of being tagged as basically disagreeable. Or are you so careful to avoid controversy that you never take a stand for a position in which you believe?

6. Are you able to space your activities? One can't operate at high speed all year long. Lefty Gomez, the former major league pitching star, once said, "A big league pitcher must bear down on every batter—but harder on some than on others."

7. Are you able to rate others effectively? This is an essential management skill. You will succeed only if you select the right people to work under and with you. The Army recognizes that leadership ability includes being able to rate others effectively. An important test during Officer Candidate School in World War II was ranking the over-all abilities of fellow officer candidates, from the most- to the least-qualified person. The composite of these rank-

ings provided an evaluation by one's peers. More important, each man's ability to rate others was easily judged by comparing his rankings with those of the group.

8. Are you performing your present duties and responsibilities to the best of your ability? Do you relate well with your superiors, colleagues, and subordinates?

9. Are you moving? Standing still may be the equivalent of going downhill. Reflect on the old Italian proverb "If there is no gain, the loss is obvious."

At this stage, you should not expect the same rate of progress which marked your early career years. Promotions become more significant, but are spaced further apart. Early advancements are often scheduled as part of a career development plan. Later promotions depend more upon availability of suitable openings, the growth and vitality of your organization, and the general economic climate.

CHAPTER 16

WEATHERING THE CRUCIAL THIRTIES

The most decisive decade of your life should be the period of your thirties. Most graduates arrive at the age of thirty armed with high hopes for the future. They have met successfully both the challenges which faced them and the expectations of their employers. The demands of the thirties will provide a rigorous test of their potential for the future. Two types of graduates emerge from this period: those who have reached their ceiling and those who, by meeting the challenge of the thirties, are marked for further advancement.

ROLE OF THE THIRTIES IN YOUR CAREER

In the thirties you should anticipate more responsible supervisory assignments. Your experience, your position, and your enthusiasm for your work should permit an increasingly worthwhile contribution to your employer.

Your problems will become more difficult and less tangible. Your solutions will affect not only you, but also your employer, fellow employees, and the general public.

Your role will become increasingly public. At the start of your career, only a few people knew of your work. In the thirties the quality of your work is observed by a growing number of subordinates, colleagues, supervisors, and customers.

Geographical relocation may become

necessary. Successful sales managers grow through assignment to more complex branch offices; school superintendents move to larger school systems in more heavily populated areas; and government officials find the top positions located in capital cities.

Relocation tests a person's enthusiasm for his career. Potential executives often must move when a good opportunity presents itself or be regarded as unambitious. Fortunately, the complications of moving are usually compensated for by an accompanying raise in salary or increase in responsibilities. Many employers pay all moving expenses in connection with relocation. Kaiser Steel, for example, will even purchase at market value the houses of men transferred at company request.

In your thirties, people as individuals and in groups hold the key to your progress. Ability to work with people becomes increasingly important, as is seen from the amount of time an executive spends working with people.*

Perhaps the most significant change in executive work—and the cause of a great deal of the extra work—is the fact that it involves more and more contacts with more and more individuals. . . . Now that "committee management" has become so much the rule, the average executive spends roughly six of his eight office hours talking with other executives in meetings and conferences, and he would be considered an odd bird indeed if he went out for lunch by himself. The other two hours are not spent in solitary contemplation; they are no more than the sum of a few minutes here and there between meetings and the ringing of the telephone.

You will have to learn to delegate authority. Don't be surprised if you find this difficult. A top industrial trainer re-

* William H. Whyte, Jr., "How Hard Executives Work," *Fortune,* January, 1954, p. 109.

cently commented, "Top executives are all too often unwilling to delegate authority and their lower subordinates often hesitate to assume this responsibility." Deliberate effort and constant practice are usually required to develop his skill.

An important factor in your progress may be a superior who not only recommends you for advancement, but also pushes for your promotion. Your supervisor's loyalty to you is directly related to your loyalty to him.

With experience and personal development, your fund of professional knowledge increases. This knowledge provides the foundation for your career. Don't be misled, however, by the thought that knowledge alone guarantees advancement. Frequently persons with great skill fail to become leaders in their field. Babe Ruth, considered by many to be the greatest baseball player of all time, never realized his goal of becoming a Big League manager. By contrast, Joe McCarthy, who won seven pennants in eight years as manager of the New York Yankees, spent his playing career in the minor leagues.

Most middle-management positions carry a specific salary range. Each position is classified according to its difficulty and its worth to the employer.

Although every position in an organization carries a firm salary range, in the thirties salary begins to reflect individual merit. Graduates with the best records reach the top of their salary range sooner than others. When they approach the top of a salary scale, consideration of promotion follows.

Evaluation of salary progress is difficult. Professional etiquette does not permit any discussion of your salary with colleagues. If in doubt, learn who controls your salary and talk with him about your progress. Avoid asking for a raise. A busy executive will not share your concern about your stock of monthly bills. Rather, set an appointment in advance with the announced goal of talking about your performance and your future. This permits preconference attention to this subject by your executive. Salary may be discussed very naturally during this interview.

SHOULD YOU SWITCH POSITIONS?

Before seriously considering a change of employers, consider the advantages of remaining in your present position:

1. Stay with your employer to take advantage of the growing tendency to promote from within. Many concerns hire graduates only at the entry level. *Fortune* studied 900 executives and discovered that 33 per cent had never worked for another organization. Furthermore, 27 per cent had worked for only one other employer. Only 23 per cent had worked for three or more employers.*
2. Stay with your employer to retain the benefits of seniority. Years of experience build up a rich knowledge of your employer and increase your worth to him and the value of the contribution you are able to make. Seniority also affects your retirement, sick benefits, vacations, and other fringe benefits. Low seniority in a new organization increases your chances of being discharged in case of a reduction in force.
3. Stay with your employer to avoid the label of "job hopper." An experienced personnel man always looks for employment continuity. He seeks employees who will stay with his organization. A few changes are acceptable; too many may create a lifelong liability.
4. Stay with your present employer if your dissatisfaction stems from restlessness. You must expect plateaus in your own advancement and promotion.

* Editors of *Fortune, The Executive Life,* Doubleday & Company, Inc., New York, 1956, p. 31.

These provide the seasoning necessary to prepare for work at the next highest level. In a survey of 3,300 graduates of The Ohio State University, one distinguishing characteristic was found among executives from all the areas studied. The highest average earnings were reported by alumni who had worked for only one employer since graduation.

5. Stay with your employer if your purpose in leaving is to escape problems. John Handy of Handy Associates feels that many alumni fail to realize that all positions and organizations have problems. In talking with graduates, he finds that many look for perfection in a position, not realizing that this search will be in vain. All positions and organizations have problems.
6. Stay with your employer if the organization has strength, stability, and creativity and you are thinking of leaving for an organization about which you are uncertain. Study growth patterns, record of service, current and future competition, population shifts, technological changes, and profits.
7. Stay with your employer if your reason for leaving is only feeling lost in the shuffle. Large firms, such as Continental Can Company, use personnel inventory records to facilitate effective utilization of manpower resources and to ensure that each employee is given the opportunity for development to his greatest potential. Continental maintains personnel records on all its 6,500 management-level employees. All inventoried persons are appraised annually on their promotion potential. A five-point scale ranging from Outstanding to Unsatisfactory is used. When nominations are sought for a management opening, Continental turns to its central personnel files. The records of all potential candidates are reviewed and the personnel files of the most likely candidates are sent to the

division having the vacancy. These employees are often considered for promotion without realizing it.

Many organizations routinely prepare a manpower inventory chart to show at a glance the status of all key employees and their positions. This chart rates each incumbent executive on both performance (often on a five-point scale running from "Exceptional" down to "Unsatisfactory") and potential for advancement on a scale which may range from "Promotable Now" down through" "Not Transferrable" to "Adjustment Case." Manpower inventory charts dramatically portray present and future management resources.

A change of employers is sometimes appropriate—in fact, may give your career a vitally needed shot-in-the-arm. Some of the situations which make a change advantageous are as follows:

1. Change positions if you are faced with a ceiling in earnings, challenge, and responsibility. One of the country's leading life insurance salesmen was formerly a very successful door-to-door salesman of household products. However, no matter how well he organized his day, the actual number of calls he could make in a day clamped an absolute ceiling on his earnings. He decided to switch his sales ability to the life insurance field and now earns ten times as much.

2. Change positions if you need to diversify your experience. Employers who seek top executives on the open market often prefer graduates who have had the broadening experience of serving in several organizations.

3. Change positions if you need to improve your acceptance. Despite frequent promotions, many young executives are handicapped because old-timers still regard them as newcomers. Many in the organization still remember the mistakes which these young executives made while they were learning. Typical is the status of the college graduate who accepts a teaching position at his alma mater.

4. Change positions if your employer's business is weak and corrective steps on your part are impossible. If your employer is not strong, his future and your future may be perilous. In the lush years of the automobile industry immediately following World War II, Manufacturer *A* earned a profit of $150 on each car produced. Manufacturer *B*'s profit was only $30. As competition increased, Manufacturer *B* was forced out of business. His employees were forced to relocate.

5. Change positions if you are certain that you are in an organization with so few future openings at levels ahead of you that your own chances for advancement are limited. Your own professional opportunities will stem from growth and expansion, retirement of older persons, or new products stemming from research. Regardless of their source, however, the volume of available opportunities directly affects your future.

If your situation is unfavorable, consider the possibility of a transfer within your organization. Moving to a new department, division, or position may result in many of the same benefits achieved by changing employers and involve fewer headaches. A transfer retains your seniority rights and other benefits. Your knowledge of your organization and its personnel continue to be assets.

HOW TO QUIT A JOB

Judgment in leaving a position can be almost as important as finesse in obtaining a job. Experience recommends that you stay on in your old position until you have found a new one. Psychologically, you will be more relaxed. Practically, employers may rate you higher if you are employed. Financially, a two- to six-month job hunt deals a devastating economic blow. The older you are, the more money you make, and the greater your specialization, the longer your change may take.

If you have received a definite and interesting job offer from another organization, discuss it with your supervisor. If you reject it, both your reputation and loyalty may be enhanced. If you accept it, your employer will have had an opportunity to make an attractive counterproposal to you. In this situation, you may receive a helpful and frank analysis of the long-range possibilities in your organization.

If you decide to leave, remember that the final impression is often the one by which you will be remembered. Discuss priorities on your assignments so that you can complete those which are important to your supervisors.

Avoid criticizing the organization or your fellow employees, either publicly or privately. An assistant sales manager accepted another job and concluded his first association with a letter intended to be helpful, but sharply critical of the organization's policies and personnel. Within six months, his new position proved to be impossible. He learned to his dismay that the sales manager whom he had been understudying had been promoted and was looking for a successor. Because of his unpleasant departure, this graduate was the one person not eligible for the opening.

CONSIDER WORKING
FOR YOURSELF

An obvious alternative in career planning is the establishment of one's own business. In the thirties, your fund of professional knowledge and your physical vigor create optimum conditions for starting in business for yourself. Your own business provides the maximum opportunity for you to benefit from your creativity, intelligence, judgment, and hard work. At the same time, the graduate considering his own business should think carefully about the breadth of h's qualifications. He should be aware also of the hazards inherent in self-employment.*

Typically, the small businessman stretches his limited capital too far, overextends credit in order to get customers, overloads himself with slow-moving stock, has no knowledge of the market or his competitors, doesn't know how to raise money when he needs it, doesn't know the principles of good management and wouldn't use them if he did.

If you go into your own business, you will be joining approximately 400,000 individuals and groups who do so annually. Only 1 out of 5 businesses lives to celebrate its tenth anniversary. Nevertheless, many new organizations are h'ghly successful. For example, consider the many new and strong electronics firms located on the fringes of Boston and on the San Francisco Peninsula.

HOW HIGH SHOULD YOU AIM?

Do you aspire to top-executive status? (Exhibit 47.) Sooner or later, you must answer this question. Studies indicate that, depending upon the definition employed, there are between 80,000 and 450,000 executives in the United States.

Eventually, every graduate reaches the point where his present job becomes his career ceiling. The fact that he moves steadily up to this point adds to the shock when he reaches it. A few missed promotions at this point may signify the end of aspirations for top management. Once a person hits his ceiling, the only possible moves are lateral transfers.

* George S. Odiorne, "How Small Business Cuts Its Throat," *Harper's Magazine,* April, 1960, p. 47.

Every man leaving the decade of his thirties must decide how far he thinks he may go, how far he wants to go, and what price he is willing to pay for further success. Failure to estimate accurately one's potential for advancement is almost as disastrous as lack of readiness to accept the obligations which accompany promotions.

As people near the top of the management ladder, other changes occur. Their financial concern may decrease. Their vocational life and community responsibilities often absorb more time and energy. At the same time, their technical knowledge of the field and specific knowledge of parts of the organization may be less than that of subordinates at the operating level.

Yet the demands on the top executive grow increasingly heavy. As a plant manager or superintendent, he was able to concentrate on a single job, complex as it may have been. As a top executive, his responsibility grows to include work with governmental agencies in order to encourage compliance with regulations or to help develop corrective legislation; cooperation in helping to build his organization's income by increasing sales and reducing costs; exploration of possibilities of mergers or expansions; consideration of reducing properties or making changes necessitated by technological advances; and his role as a leader in his profession.

As one reaches the zenith of his career, he develops a clearer appreciation of his role in society. The ability to recognize the importance and worth of other people —superiors, colleagues, subordinates, customers, friends, competitors, and even strangers—is indispensable to living a full life either personally or professionally. Lack of respect for others not only limits one's personal horizons, but also handicaps professional aspirations. The fourth Arden House conference sponsored by Columbia University emphasized the importance of recognizing those around you in these words: "There can be no doubt of the importance [of status] to human beings. . . . It appears to be a primary need of human beings to be set apart somehow from their fellows, to be accepted as different from and—in some respects—superior to others."

If you are in a supervisory capacity, much of your satisfaction may come from

Exhibit 47 PICTURE OF AN EXECUTIVE

"The successful executive typically can channel his energies effectively into his work. He meets the requirements of organizations for dedication to work and for discipline. He does not work out of a sense of guilt but out of the satisfaction he gains from accomplishing things. He tends to be the kind of person who picks up energy like a two-cycle engine through work itself.

"He not only has the emotional energy to channel into his work but also the physical stamina. Sheer survival is one of the requirements of successful executives. Those who drop off in their early forties have no chance to develop their full capacities."

David Moore, "Why Some Win, Others Lose," Nation's Business, October, 1960, p. 41.

helping younger people assume greater responsibility and develop their own talents. The executive who does not develop his successors is robbing himself of one of the great pleasures in life, and dooms his organization to mediocrity in years to come.

This book has emphasized the importance of developing principles upon which to build your life, especially your vocational life. The development of such principles will help ensure making full use of your natural abilities. You will feel satisfied in life only if you make full use of your talents. As Emerson said: "Nothing can bring you peace but yourself. Nothing can bring you peace but the triumph of principles."

APPENDIX

THE PRINCIPLES AND PRACTICES OF COLLEGE RECRUITING

This statement sets forth the basic agreements developed by college placement directors and business, industrial, and governmental recruiting officers in Canada and the United States for guidance in the practice of their profession.

GENERAL PRINCIPLES

It is in the best interests of students, colleges, and employers alike that the selection of careers be made in an objective atmosphere with complete understanding of all the facts.

Therefore, the recruiting of college students for employment by business, industry, government, and education should be carried out by the employers, students, and college authorities to serve best the following objectives:

1. To promote a wise and responsible choice of a career by the student for his own greatest satisfaction, minimum wasteful turnover, and most fruitful long-term investment of his talents for himself, for his employer, and for society.

2. To strengthen in him a high standard of integrity and a concept of similar standards in the employing organizations of the country.

3. To develop in the student an attitude of personal responsibility for his own career and advancement in it, based on performance.

4. To minimize interference with the educational processes of the college and to encourage completion of the individual's plans for further education.

PRACTICES AND PROCEDURES

Responsibilities of the employer

1. The employer should contact the Placement Office well in advance regarding desired interview dates, broad categories of

employment expected to be available, college degrees, and other pertinent requirements. He should advise promptly any change in his original request or subsequent arrangements with the Placement Office.

2. The employer should provide suitable literature to give students a true and factual picture of the employing organization. This material should be supplied in sufficient quantities and well in advance of the interviewing date.

3. When both the parent organization and subsidiary or affiliated organization conduct interviews in the same college, the respective interviewers should explain clearly their missions and the connections, both to the Placement Office and to the students.

4. Not more than two and preferably only one interviewer representing an employer should appear for each interview schedule. Arrangements for more than two interviewers should be made in advance, and only for reasons considered adequate by the Placement Office.

5. The placement or other appropriate officer of the college should be advised in advance of any plans for campus visits by the representatives of an employer, including alumni of the college, to acquaint faculty members or students with company employment activities or opportunities. Such representatives should exercise scrupulous care to avoid undue demands on the time of faculty members or students.

6. An employer who desires to contact an individual student at the time of his interview visit should communicate with the individual well in advance with a notice to the Placement Office.

7. Prior to or at the time of the offer of employment, the employer should clearly explain to the Placement Office and to the student all conditions of employment.

8. The interviewer should be punctual. He should tell the Placement Office when he will arrive as well as his expected departure time. Every effort should be made to avoid last minute cancellations.

9. The interviewer should very carefully follow the interview time schedule agreed upon with the Placement Office.

10. As soon as possible following an interview, the employer should communicate with the student and the Placement Office concerning the outcome of the interview.

11. The employer should give the student reasonable time to consider his offer, and in no case should the student be pressured into making a decision concerning employment.

12. If the employer invites a student to visit his premises for further discussion of employment, the visit should be arranged to interfere as little as possible with class schedules. He should explain what expenses will be paid, how, and when. Invitations for this purpose should be made only on an individual basis and the employer should avoid elaborate entertaining or overselling.

13. The employer should not offer a student special payments, gifts, bonuses, or other inducements, nor should he compensate or favor a third party to prevail upon the student to accept an employment offer.

14. Employers should not raise offers already made, except when such action can be clearly justified as sound industrial relations practice; such as, when an increase in hiring rate is required on an over-all basis to reflect salary adjustments in the employing organization.

15. The employer should keep the Placement Office informed concerning his interest in particular students and his negotiations with them.

16. When a student has declined a job offer, the employer should accept that decision as final. If for any reason the employer wishes to re-establish contact with the student, he should do so only through the Placement Office.

17. The employer should engage each student who has accepted his offer except when failure to do so is the direct result of contingencies explained during the interview or unavoidable economic factors not foreseen when the offer was made.

Responsibilities of the college

1. As part of its general obligation for the development of the student, the college should accept responsibility for stimulation of his thinking about his career objectives and for assistance in overcoming handicaps which may hinder his progress toward objectives appropriate for him. Competent counseling services should be provided for this purpose, available to individual students.

2. The Placement Office should inform employers concerning the number of students available for interview in the several curricula and the dates of graduation. This information should be sent as soon as it is available.

3. The Placement Office should announce to students early in the school year which employers will interview students and when. The Placement Office should make such revised announcements from time to time as may be necessary.

4. The Placement Office should make employment literature available to students and faculty.

5. When an employer is looking for graduates in several fields (i.e., engineering, psychology, physics), the Placement Office should issue announcements to all qualified students concerned, and, so far as practicable, should schedule interviews for those who express interest.

6. The Placement Office should not restrict the number of interviews per student, except as necessary to discourage indiscriminate "shopping."

7. The college should provide adequate space and facilities for quiet and private interviews.

8. The Placement Office should provide interviewers with available records of those students in whom they are interested.

9. The Placement Office should arrange for interviewers to meet faculty members who know students personally and can provide information about their work and qualifications.

10. The Placement Officer and faculty members should counsel students but should not unduly influence them in the selection of jobs.

11. The Placement Office should make certain that students are acquainted with this statement of "Principles and Practices of College Recruiting."

Responsibilities of the student

1. In seeking company interviews, the student should recognize his responsibility to analyze his interests and abilities and consider carefully his career objective and appropriate ways of meeting it. He should read available literature and consult other sources for information about the employer and organize his thoughts in order that he may intelligently ask and answer questions.

2. The student should contact the Placement Office well in advance regarding desired interviews or cancellations.

3. The student should use care in filling out such forms as may be requested in preparation for interviews.

4. In his interviews, the student should recognize that he is representing his college, as well as himself, and should be punctual and thoroughly businesslike in his conduct.

5. The student should promptly acknowledge an invitation to visit an employer's premises. He should accept an invitation only when he is sincerely interested in exploring employment with that employer.

6. When a student is invited to visit an employer's premises at the employer's expense, he should include on his expense report only those costs which pertain to the trip. If he visits several employers on the same trip, costs should be prorated among them.

7. As soon as the student determines that he will not accept an offer, he should immediately notify the employer.

8. The student should not continue to present himself for interviews after he has accepted an employment offer.

9. Acceptance of an employment offer by the student should be made in good faith and with the sincere intention of honoring his employment commitment.

10. The student should keep the Placement Office advised concerning his employment negotiations in accordance with the policy of his Placement Office.

INDEX